The Scripture Unbroken

The
Scripture
Unbroken

BY

LESTER J. KUYPER

WILLIAM B. EERDMANS PUBLISHING COMPANY

Copyright © 1978 by Wm. B. Eerdmans Publishing Co.
255 Jefferson Ave. SE, Grand Rapids, Mich. 49503
All rights reserved
Printed in the United States of America

Library of Congress Cataloging in Publication Data

Kuyper, Lester Jacob, 1904-
    The Scripture unbroken.

    1. Bible. N.T.—Relation to the Old Testament.
    2. Covenants (Theology)—Biblical teaching. I. Title.
BS2387.K84   220.6'3   77-26854
ISBN 0-8028-1734-3

FOREWORD

T HERE ARE SEVERAL GOOD BOOKS ON THE RELA-
tion of the Old and New Testaments, the unity of
revelation, and the use of the Old Testament in the
New. But there is no book like this one, both because of its content and because of the distinctive
approach of the author.

The first two chapters of this volume cover
rather familiar ground, albeit in a fresh way. Rapid-
ly, however, new ground is broken and themes are
discussed which are usually not found in a book of
this type. Some of these chapters have already appeared in essay form in theological journals such as
the *Reformed Review, Interpretation,* and the *Scottish Journal of Theology.* They are expressive of
life-long studies and concerns of Lester Kuyper and
have made their mark in the scholarly world. A
number of these essays have been cited in recent
commentaries and biblical studies. Here they are
brought together with several completely new chapters in order to elucidate and illustrate the central
thesis of the book—the continuity of the two Testaments in the light of the concept of fulfillment.

The critical scholar should not be put off by

what might appear at first glance to be a facile and superficial harmonizing of the two Testaments. Nor should the more popular reader assume that we have here a simple, uncritical approach to the relation of the Old and New Testaments. Lester Kuyper is too careful and perceptive a scholar to overlook and gloss over some formidable difficulties in this regard. He approaches these questions—as well as those of the nature of God and his dealings with mankind—with refreshing openness and honesty. He is quite aware of the problems and refuses to provide neat, harmonizing solutions. At the same time, he comes to these great themes of covenant and history, righteousness and salvation, grace and truth, suffering and repentance, with a profound reverence for the God of the covenant who has revealed himself in the Scriptures and ultimately in Jesus Christ.

This is more than a survey of the relation of the Testaments and the nature of the Scriptures. We have here also studies in depth of key issues concerning the character and ways of God. Although the author does not attempt to give us a full-blown doctrine of God, any thological treatment of this subject should reckon with the insights provided in this volume. Lester Kuyper is by no means a-theological in his approach to biblical studies, but he is not intimidated by classical dogmatic terminology and concepts. In fact, a not-so-secret item on his agenda is to challenge systematic theologians to re-examine some of their ways of thinking about and describing God and his ways with the world.

Lester Kuyper has a hearty respect for tradition, and for his own Reformed tradition in particular, but this does not prevent him from criticizing various time-honored theological notions, especially in regard to God. Fortunately, there are dogmatic theologians who are willing to respond to this challenge. One is Hendrikus Berkhof, the distinguished theologian from the University of Leiden in the Netherlands, who has expressed gratitude for "Kuyper's concern to enrich dogmatic theology by fresh biblical insights." He continues, "His biblical scholarship is accompanied by a wealth of dogmatic knowledge that is as rare among biblical specialists as is the reverse among dogmatic theologians" ("The (Un)-Changeability of God" in *Grace Upon Grace* [Eerdmans, 1975], pp. 21-22. See also Berkhof's reference to Kuyper in the former's *Christelijk Geloof*, p. 150).

What makes this book unique, however, is not so much its content, valuable as it is, but the character and outlook of the author. Fortunate are those who have known the author as a student, colleague, or friend. For them many of the lines of these chapters will speak with special force because they reflect so vividly the personality and convictions of the author. This is true in some measure of any book, but in the case of Lester Kuyper we are dealing with a Christian gentleman and scholar of peculiar charm, warmth, and wisdom.

Those readers who do not know the author personally I would like to direct to the biographical essay in the volume of essays presented to him on the occasion of his retirement after teaching thirty-five years at Western Theological Seminary (*Grace*

Upon Grace, pp. 9-17). I would add only that although those lovable qualities which have endeared him to so many friends throughout the years do not always shine through the printed page, it should be obvious to anyone who reads this book carefully that the author is not only a fine scholar, but is at the same time a scholar with a pastor's heart, one who is concerned to share his understanding of the God of the Scriptures not only with scholars but with all the people of God.

Western Theological Seminary   I. JOHN HESSELINK

CONTENTS

PREFACE

A LABEL ON A PACKAGE OF MERCHANDISE INTENDS to be descriptive and attractive. We observe that modern marketing makes special effort to present its goods in forms and designs that will attract the customer. And special study is given to the name or label by which the product is to be known and sold. Old commonplace products such as soda water become more appealing attached to a slogan such as, "You like it and it likes you."

The title of this book, *The Scripture Unbroken*, is an attempt to present an old study under a new label. The subject of biblical hermeneutics, or the relationship between the Old and New Testaments, has been discussed in many biblical introductions, in biblical dictionaries and journals, and in books on this subject. In these studies the most common word used to describe the continuity of the Old Testament in the New is "fulfillment." This word in both verbal and nounal forms appears frequently in the New Testament, whose authors often relate their writings to the Old Testament by means of a formula, "That it might be fulfilled what was written by the prophet." As this book will demonstrate, especially in Chapter I, "The Old Testament Used by New Testament Writers," the use of "fulfillment" in the New Testament indicated that the inspired writers held the Old Testament to be incomplete in itself and believed that it was finding its completion and consummation in the advent of Christ and the establishing of the church through the outpouring of the Holy Spirit. For these phenomena of completion the New Testament uses the word "fulfillment."

Another word, although less used than fulfillment, is the Greek verb *luein* with the negative, "not to destroy, not to break." This word appears three times in the Gospel of John to indicate that the Scripture cannot be broken (10:35); that the law of Moses may not be broken (7:23); and that the Jews accused Jesus of breaking the sabbath (5:18). In the Gospel of Matthew Jesus declares that he did not come to break down the law and the prophets but to fulfill them (5:17), and that anyone breaking one of the least significant commandments shall be accounted least in the kingdom of heaven (5:19). For the Scripture or the law to be unbroken therefore serves as an interesting and informing synonym for fulfillment of the Scripture.

A brief study of the above references will cast some light not only on our understanding of what the unbroken Scripture means but also on the idea of fulfillment. In the context of John 10:35 Jesus contends with the Jews about their charge of blasphemy against him, for they allege that he made himself equal with God. Jesus appeals to Psalm 82 in which God is denouncing rulers for their miscarriage of justice. Even though they are without knowledge and walk in darkness, yet they are addressed, "You are gods, sons of the Most High, all of you" (Ps. 82:6). The point which Jesus makes here is that since God called rulers, unjust though they were, gods and sons of the Most High, it is not blasphemous for him to call himself the Son of God. The principle that validates this conclusion is expressed thus: "And scripture cannot be broken." This principle asserts that the teaching of the Old Testament has validity which is applicable and regulative for all times. The validity of the Old Testament carries on beyond its own time; it cannot be broken, that is, become null and void.

In John 7:23 Jesus speaks about the Jews' practice of circumcising on the sabbath so that the law of Moses which required that circumcision take place on the eighth day might not be broken. The "not breaking" of the law of Moses which both Jesus and the Jews endorsed meant that the law of circumcision established many centuries before was still valid. In the Jews' accusation that Jesus "was breaking the sabbath" (5:18) because of his healing the man at the pool of Bethzatha, it is clear that the law of the sabbath which forbad work was being regarded as authoritative and binding, even as the other laws of the Old Testament.

In the Sermon on the Mount (Mt. 5:17,19) Jesus emphatically declares that he did not come to "break down" the law and the prophets, that is, the Old Testament, but he came to fulfill. Here "to break down" is followed by its antonym "to fulfill." In the nineteenth verse the "breaking-down" of the least commandment and the teaching of that attitude toward the Old Testament are contrasted with the doing and the teaching of the commandment. The breaking-down would be the same as not-doing the commandment, or not-breaking-down would be doing the commandment, and this implies that Jesus regarded the teachings of the Old Testament as authoritative guides for conduct. The not-breaking-down, or the fulfilling, of the law and the prophets therefore means that the Old Testament which was God's word for ancient Israel has meaning and authority for those who are of the kingdom of heaven.

From the above we may observe that the unbroken-scripture concept clearly insists upon the Old Testament's being God's message and guide for each generation. The title, *The Scripture Unbroken,* may serve us as a meaningful approach toward the Old and New Testaments in that the entire Bible has validity for our faith and life, even as the Old Testament had validity for Jesus and the apostles. Key concepts and themes in the Old Testament recur in the New. This is the author's attitude toward the Bible, and he invites the reader of this book to share it as he enters the fellowship of study of the relationship between the Old and New Testaments.

LESTER J. KUYPER

CHAPTER I

THE OLD TESTAMENT USED BY NEW TESTAMENT WRITERS

Before he gives any thought to the origin of the Bible, a child reared in a Christian home learns that the Bible has two parts which are equally revered as sacred and inspired. He regards this two-part Book as one of the established facts of life, much like the law of gravity. However, as through experience and education he reaches into the world about him, he learns that the Bible is not like a law of nature or a date in history. He learns further that those who honor the Bible esteem it with various degrees of appreciation. And when he encounters Jews he may be surprised to observe that their Bible has only the first part, the Old Testament. If not by meeting Jews or by seeing their Bible, every Christian will soon or late note that the two divisions of the Bible are not the author's device for arrangement of material, but that each part is the basis for a distinct, sèparate faith. If then the Old Testament is the basis for the Jewish faith, the question is not far distant why it should be a part of the Christian Scriptures. Thus arises the problem concerning the relationship of the Old Testament to the Christian faith.

1

Perhaps we should rephrase the problem to inquire what the relationship between the Old Testament and the New Testament might be. This problem has especially engaged the minds of biblical scholars during the past three decades; one may say that this is one of the most important problems in biblical research today. In classrooms, at meetings of biblical societies, and in learned journals the relationship of the two Testaments is critically examined. Solutions for the problem, if any are reached, carry certain qualifications and reservations to indicate the virtual impossibility of finding a solution for the complex problem.

Since both Testaments comprise the Bible we accept as the basis for our faith, no difficulty should dissuade us from attempting a discussion for an understanding and clarification of the problem. Surely, in view of what we now know about the problem, we should not hope to arrive at a solution fully satisfying to all. However, a discussion carefully undertaken may disclose insights and interpretations of the Bible that far outweigh a solution fully or partially achieved.

The Background of the New Testament

In every book and often on every page the New Testament acknowledges the Old Testament as the authoritative Word of God. We can readily observe this in the life and teaching of Jesus. When he was assailed by the tempter he quoted the Old Testament as authority for rejecting the temptation (Mt. 4:4-10). Both Jesus and his opponents, whether the devil or the Jews, accepted the Old Testament as the authority to which appeals could be made. In his debate with the Pharisees about the sabbath, Jesus used the Old Testament to refute his opponents (Mt. 12:1-8). To the perplexed disciples on the way to Emmaus Jesus explained his mission by interpreting the law of Moses, the prophets, and the psalms (Lk. 24:44). The purpose and goal of his ministry was to fulfill the law and the prophets (Mt. 5:17).

Jesus' attack on the interpreters of the Old Testament must in no instance be regarded as an attack on the Old Testament itself. His intent was to liberate the Old Testament from the bondage of legalism which prevailed in Judaism. He appealed to the spirit of the law rather than to the letter, for the spirit of the Old Testament was the living authority of the Book. The conflict between Jesus and his opponents bespoke a profound respect and understanding of the Old Testament that produced in the disciples an attitude of mind which could, on the one hand, accept the ancient Scriptures as authoritative and, on the other hand, interpret them according to the spirit and not according to the letter. In the school of Jesus the disciples learned freedom with reverence: freedom from any form of legalism, and reverence for the living Word of God. Jesus set the standard for the proper appeal to and the use of the Old Testament.

The people's comment that Jesus taught with authority and not as the scribes (Mt. 7:28-29) indicates that Jesus' method of teaching and interpretation was contrasted with methods well known to the people. Different methods and types of interpretations were indeed current among the Jews, and were without doubt known to Jesus and to the writers of the New Testament. For convenience we may list them as the rabbinic method, the allegorical method of Philo, and the *pesher* method used at Qumran.

The rabbinic method is well described by the seven rules of Hillel, a renowned rabbi of the first century.[1] It included principles of analogy, of generalization, and of context, and may be recognized as common sense principles for understanding any kind of literature. In the application of the rules, however, we observe that rabbinic exegesis did not restrict itself to rules but indulged in much freedom and in fantasy. Clever and pious combinations of texts produced some interesting results. An example of this concerns the rock which Moses struck with his staff to produce water in the wilderness. The first mention of the rock is in Exodus 17, and since the rock also appears in Numbers 20, the conclusion is drawn that the rock journeyed with Israel to serve as a fountain of water which is also mentioned in Numbers 21:16-18. The rabbis therefore spoke of a movable fountain the size of a beehive which was created on the sixth day to be used for Israel's wilderness wanderings. Paul no doubt alluded to this rabbinic teaching in I Corinthians 10 when he identifies this rock with Christ.

Philo of Alexandria, a Jew of the dispersion not under the control of rabbinic tradition, interpreted the Old Testament through Platonic

4

concepts of Greek philosophy.[2] The world of things and of history is but the shadow or form of the world of ideas. The so-called material things of the Old Testament, such as people, places, and events, were interpreted through allegory to mean something that belonged to the world of ideas. With this method Philo could change the content of the Old Testament law and history into the ideas of the spirit world. Something akin to Philo's allegory is found in Paul's use of the law of the threshing ox (I Cor. 9:9-10), from which Paul derives the principle that the workman is entitled to his hire. Allegory and typology will be discussed later and therefore it is not necessary here to examine the contrast and similarities between the New Testament method and the allegorical method

The Qumran pesher has become well known in biblical studies especially because of the Habakkuk scroll found with other Dead Sea scrolls.[3] The author presents a commentary on short portions of Habakkuk, often with the introductory formula, *peshrô 'al*, "its *pesher*, interpretation, concerns." He intends to show that the words of the Old Testament prophet were then in process of fulfillment. The prophet spoke in a mystery beyond his own understanding, but God reveals that mystery to the teacher of righteousness who communicates the full interpretation to the Qumran community. At first glance it seems that liberties are taken with the Old Testament text, but on closer examination these so-called liberties fall within a framework of exegetical rules which make use of changes of letters, text variations, and

5

synonyms. The author's main purpose is to demonstrate that the words of the prophet have their
meaning in the experience of the Qumran sect.
The fulfillment of Habakkuk is seen in the coming
of the Romans, the wickedness of the priest, and
the appearance of the Teacher of Righteousness.
The comment on Habakkuk 2:4, "The righteous
shall live by his faith," points out that the doers of
the law escape judgment because of their toil and
their faith in the Teacher of Righteousness. The
Qumran pesher is therefore much like the method
of the New Testament writers in that both of them
find the Old Testament reaching fulfillment, the
one in the Teacher of Righteousness and the
Qumran community, and the other in Jesus of Nazareth and the church.

From the above survey of three types of interpretation current at the time the New Testament
was written, we can easily surmise that the writers
of gospels and epistles were conversant with some
or all methods then in vogue. They would therefore use whatever method would best serve their
purpose. Furthermore, since the readers were for
the most part Jews, either those within Hebrew
culture or those in the Gentile world, the authors
of the New Testament would use language and
thought forms, as well as methods of exegesis,
which readily communicated the significance of
Jesus Christ and the Christian church.

Our discussion to this point reveals that in
their attitude toward the Old Testament the
writers of the New Testament followed the example of Jesus in not being subject to any school of

the scribes and yet being free to use methods, thought forms, and language of these schools. We may observe that these writers combine freedom and bondage: freedom from established methods of interpretation and their established results, freedom for searching the Old Testament to discover the dynamic meaning of the Word of God, and yet bondage to the use of the thought forms of their times.

In the many references to the Old Testament we observe that no one Old Testament text is cited. Quotations are taken primarily from the Septuagint (LXX), the Greek Old Testament then in common use by the Christians. In many instances the LXX and the Hebrew texts agree so that a preference for one or the other cannot be determined. However, several other examples show a preference for the LXX against the Hebrew text. The opposite is much less frequently true.

In the frequent instances where the quotations diverge from both the LXX and the Hebrew texts they may be taken from the Aramaic Targum, which was a free, commentary-type translation which came into use because of the inability of Aramaic-speaking Jews to understand Hebrew. Citations may also have been derived from a collection of *Testimonia,* now recognized as a compilation of Old Testament texts in use among Christians.[4] Other quotations may have been a free rendition of one or more passages which in effect retained the sense if not the literal exactness of the text. The variety of sources for quotations should in no wise detract from the impression that the

7

New Testament writers regarded the Old Testament as of paramount importance for understanding the coming of Christ and the establishing of the church.

The many Old Testament quotations and references we encounter in the New Testament were designed to achieve one goal: fulfillment. Because of its frequent occurrence in the gospels and the Acts, the Greek verb *pleroun,* "to fulfill," becomes our keyword for unlocking the significance of events attending the birth and ministry of Jesus. Fulfillment was taking place. The Old Testament word from God had been spoken; it had not yet become an event in history. The transformation of the spoken Word into the observable Event was being realized; Word was being fulfilled in Event.

We do well, in this setting, to observe that the Hebrew noun *dabhar,* commonly translated "word," embodies a two-fold sense: word and event. The first meaning is much like our understanding of "word," a vehicle of communication as in the prologue to the decalogue, "God spoke all these words saying," or like the "words of the wisemen" (Eccles. 12:11). The second meaning may be seen in the Hebrew title for Chronicles, *debharê hayyamim,* "The events of the days." *Dabar* is on the one hand the message which God places in the prophet's mouth (Jer. 1:9), and on the other hand the inspiring event from God which happens to the prophet (Jer. 1:4, 11, 13).

The sequence of spoken word and realized event quite naturally involved fulfillment. The spoken word often took on the sense of promise which awaited the actualization of the word. The word spoken to Abraham that his seed should inherit the land became a realized event under Joshua (cf. Ps. 105:8, 42). The word of God spoken by Joshua against Jericho also reached fulfillment (Josh. 6:26; I Kings 16:34). The word of promise or of doom looked forward to realization. The blessing and the curse are more than outbursts of temperamental moods, for the words thus spoken must finally reach fulfillment. "Word," therefore, when its Old Testament significance is fully comprehended, embodies expectancy, actualization, and fulfillment.

This brief digression on *dabar* intends to set the background of "to fulfill" in clear perspective. It shows first of all that God proclaimed his word to his people in the Old Testament. This living word reached into the experience of his people Israel who were delivered from the bondage of Egypt and made the people of God under Moses. They were the ones through whom the word addressed to the patriarchs reached fulfillment especially during the reigns of David and Solomon. However, the tragic humiliation of being a subject people during the exile converted the past glory of Israel into a mocking dream. Yet in that state of humiliation prophets arose to proclaim God's word anew. God had not abandoned his people, for another fulfillment of his word was to take place in the restoration of the exiles to their homeland. God's word would not return to him empty, but it would accomplish the divine purpose of changing Israel's captivity into the freedom of living in the blessed land promised to the fathers. However, as the generations passed, this freedom was only partially realized since first the Greeks and later the Romans made Palestine a vassal state. The Old Testament comes to a close looking and hoping for the time when God will again act and when the promised word of God will become event.

As the evangelists took up their pens to elaborate on the theme "fulfillment," they stood, we should clearly remember, some years after Pentecost. No doubt they were among the early disciples who frequently assembled to rehearse the words and deeds of Jesus. The death and resurrection of their Lord had indeed given new dimension to their understanding of what Jesus had come to fulfill. The first preaching of the disciples as recorded in the Acts was to make clear to the Jews that the Old Testament had been fulfilled in the resurrection of Christ. Moreover, the outpouring of the Spirit at Pentecost was an additional fulfillment of the prophets. Within the fellowship of an early church that diligently pondered the Old Testament the evangelists developed the theme of fulfillment, a subject of primary interest to all Jews of that time.

Fulfillment in Matthew, Chapters 1-2

Let us select the Gospel of Matthew to observe how the author uses the Old Testament references. In the stories concerning Jesus' birth we are given five instances in which the prophets were being fulfilled. Four are cited with the expression that all

10

this was done that it might be fulfilled what was *spoken* by the prophet; one has, as it was *written* by the prophet (2:5).

The first (1:22-23) is the well-known "virgin" passage which cites Isaiah's message to King Ahaz (Is. 7:14). The king, who greatly feared the nations of Israel and Syria, was assured by a sign that the threat of these nations would vanish. The promised sign was that a young woman would bear a son and that before the lad had reached the age of knowing right and wrong Israel and Syria would have become weak and harmless. The son was to be given the name Immanuel, "God with us," to indicate that God was with Judah to protect her against her foes. Two features in the Isaiah passage are used by Matthew: the birth of a son from a virgin, and the name Immanuel. The LXX *parthenos*, "virgin," instead of the Hebrew *'almah*, "young woman," offered a ready association with the Virgin Mary; and the name Immanuel, although never used for Jesus later, fittingly described the birth of Jesus as God coming into close fellowship with his people. We should note that the other elements in the Isaiah account, such as the fear of Ahaz, and the threat of hostile nations and their impending doom, are not used; they had no bearing upon the virgin birth of Jesus.

The second citation (2:6), "And you, O Bethlehem, in the land of Judah, are by no means least among the rulers of Judah; for from you shall come a ruler who will govern my people Israel," is taken from Micah 5:2,4 [1,3]. In answer to Herod's question, the chief priests and scribes used

11

this text to show that the Christ was to be born in Bethlehem. Here we have a sample of the method used by the scribes to determine the fulfillment of the Old Testament. The prophet saw Judah under the power of Assyria, but only for a time, for out of Bethlehem, a small place among the clans of Judah, a mighty ruler would arise. He would become the shepherd to care for Israel, and the scattered brethren would again return to be with the people of Israel. Since the LXX compares Bethlehem's ruler with the rulers of Judah, instead of the clans of Judah, this passage served well to awaken hopes for the overthrow of the feared and hated rulers of Judah, such as King Herod. This citation omits the name Ephrathah and inserts the land of Judah to make the reference to Bethlehem clear. Other matters in Micah, such as the rule of the oppressive power, the antiquity of the expected ruler, and the return of the scattered brethren are not included, apparently because they do not serve any use in answering Herod's question.

The third citation, "Out of Egypt have I called my son" (2:15), is taken from Hosea 11:1. In this context the prophet is looking back into Israel's history to observe that God loved the young nation Israel as a father loves his son. God called his son out of Egypt to become his people. Even though Israel often turned away from God to worship other gods, yet God continued to love his son and taught him to walk as a nation. He healed the waywardness of his son and provided for him. Such was God's fatherly relationship to Israel. Matthew picks up two references, those to Egypt and son, from the prophet. Since Jesus was in Egypt in his infancy, it was easy to draw the parallel with Israel's sojourn there. And it is very obvious that Jesus was God's son in a unique sense (cf. 3:17). Again we may observe that details such as the waywardness of Israel and the instruction given Israel are not relevant to the comparison and therefore are not mentioned. The important point is the Father's loving care for his Son.

The fourth citation, "A voice was heard in Ramah, wailing and loud lamentation, Rachel weeping for her children; she refused to be consoled, because they were no more" (2:18), is taken from Jeremiah 31:15. The prophet describes the plight of captive Israel in terms of the weeping at Ramah. Rachel, the mother of the tribe of Benjamin, is in great sorrow because her children have been taken away into captivity. However, the prophet offers consolation in that Rachel's children shall again return to their country. The apparent connection between the weeping of the mothers in Bethlehem because of Herod's slaying the innocents and the weeping of Rachel for her descendants lost in exile can be noted readily. Since Rachel's tomb was believed to be near Bethlehem it was easy to relate Rachel's weeping with that of the Bethlehem mothers. Although the circumstances which brought on these tragedies were different, and although the subsequent word of the prophet's consolation is not used in this reference, the weeping of mothers for lost children is still a most striking parallel.

The final citation in Matthew's birth narrative

is, "And he went and dwelt in a city called Nazareth, that what was spoken by the prophets might be fulfilled, 'He shall be called a Nazarene'" (2:23). One searches the Old Testament in vain for a reference containing these words. We can only conjecture that Matthew is alluding to Old Testament words whose root letters correspond with Nazareth so that a similarity in root or sound suggests the idea of fulfillment in this instance. In Leviticus 21:12 the anointed priest is called the *nezer,* one consecrated to his God by the anointing oil. Possibly the reference is to Isaiah 11:1 where *netzer* is a branch from the root of Jesse, apparently an allusion to the coming Davidic ruler. Another possible reference is *netzîrê,* "the preservers" of Israel (Is. 49:6), the ones who survived the exile in Babylon. Since we have no reference to a particular passage we cannot determine the historical setting as in the other references. The assonance of Nazareth with a few Hebrew words may have been the means of finding a fulfillment in Jesus' living in Nazareth.[5]

To summarize the study of the birth-narrative citations, we observe that two are in the future tense, looking ahead for fulfillment, one describes a past event, and another a present tragedy. All, whatever their distinctions in tenses, come under the common category of fulfillment. Further, we note that parallelisms are drawn between the Old Testament and the New Testament event; details of the Old Testament not usable in the parallelism are bypassed. Also, slight divergences in the words of the texts appear. These may be due to the state

14

of flux which the Old Testament text was in at that time. The intent of these citations is clearly to establish connections between events at the birth of Jesus, and words and events of the Old Testament.

No one word can adequately define the method of the evangelist. The best that comes to mind is "allusion." The word must be understood in its etymological structure as playing at something. Here play must not be understood in the sense of frivolity or irresponsibility, but rather-in the sense of serious probing into a matter, much like the probing of a scientist into elements before him. Allusion may be a kind of serious research conducted according to commonly accepted procedure. The early Christian scholars such as Matthew, much like their Jewish contemporaries, zealously worked and reworked Old Testament passages to draw out finds that would have special meaning for the new age which Christ, through his resurrection and by the sending of the Holy Spirit, had introduced.

Other Fulfillment References

The citations in the birth narrative of Matthew may well serve as examples of methods used in the gospels and indeed in the entire New Testament. We observe some rather accurate quotations of the Old Testament text (Mt. 12:18-21) in which the ministry of Jesus finds its description in terms of the ministry of the Servant (Is. 42:1-4). Or we note that, by the use of allusion, words and ideas and events from more than one source are brought to bear on an event, as in the case of the thirty pieces of silver in the betrayal narrative (Mt. 27:5-10). Words and phrases referring to the thirty pieces of silver, the price, the potter, and the casting of the silver into the temple are found in Zechariah (11:12-14); and the potter, the place for burial, and the buying of the field are taken from Jeremiah (ch. 19,32). The latter references account for the quotation's being ascribed to Jeremiah. The diverse elements found in these two prophets serve as fitting allusions to the betrayal and events associated with it.

The perplexing quotation in Matthew 2:23, noted above, suggests that some references to the Old Testament are less obvious or more subtle than verbatim quotations. C. H. Dodd is of the opinion that the early Christians concentrated their studies especially on certain portions of the Old Testament, especially the prophets and the psalms.[6] And if one may judge from all references, direct and indirect, then within the prophets and the psalms certain portions become prominent: Isaiah 6-11 and 40-55; Psalms 22 and 69 in reference to the suffering of Christ; and also Joel 2-3, Zechariah 9-14, and Daniel 7 and 12. These so-called "favorite" sections became the fertile background to which the writers of the early church turned to find allusions and parallels to the coming of Christ and the outpouring of the Holy Spirit upon the church.

In addition to allusions, as described above, we note that writers employ typology as another method of relating the New Testament to the Old.

The apostle Paul made the events of the wilderness wandering serve as types for the instruction and warning of believers who were living in the final age (**cf.** I Cor. 10:11). The word "type" is not often used (only twice by Paul) to point out some Old Testament event, yet the idea that the events of the past serve as types or prefigurations of New Testament events or persons is readily discernible. Thus it is that Adam, Moses, David, and the sacrifice of the paschal lamb are looked upon as types of Christ. Moreover, the exodus especially and the faith of Abraham are frequently referred to as models for understanding the Christian experience. Typology often appears without the formal "that it might be fulfilled" as in the cases of allusion. Yet much like the allusions, the person or event in the past is a type that finds significant fulfillment in either Christ or his church.

The Epistle to the Hebrews employs typology most frequently. Not only are Aaron, Moses, Joshua, and Melchizedek types of Christ, but also the tabernacle in the wilderness and the ancient cult of Israel prefigure the sacrificial atonement of Christ. Moreover, the heroes of the faith (ch. 11) serve as typical and instructive examples for the encouragement of believers in their pilgrimage. From reading the Epistle to the Hebrews one gathers the impression that the Old Testament with its events, persons, and institutions was God's prearranged plan for redemption that found complete realization in the priestly ministry of Christ and in his sacrifice.

Typology, as defined by Eichrodt, regards per-

17

sons, events, and institutions as divinely established models of corresponding realities in the New Testament salvation events.[7] The correspondence between the Testaments should in every case be restricted to those points designated by the author. For example, in the correspondence between Moses and Christ in II Corinthians 3:7ff., Paul calls attention to two factors, the *diakonia* and the *doxa* (ministry and glory). Only according to these does Moses here serve as the type for Christ. In both the *diakonia* and the *doxa* Christ far excels Moses the type. In some cases the type illustrates a contrast such as that between Adam and Christ in which Adam's sin brought on guilt and death and Christ's justification brought on righteousness and life (**cf.** Rom. 5:15ff.). In every case the type is but the preliminary stage of the plan for salvation; the realization of the plan is reached in Christ.

Since typology has points of similarity with allegory, a method much used in the history of interpretation, we should clarify the distinctions between the two. This is all the more necessary since in Galatians 4:21-26 Paul expressly states that the narrative of Abraham, his two sons, and his two wives is an allegory to represent two covenants, the covenant of Judaism which is slavery, and that of the church which is free. In what sense does Paul use allegory here? One might suppose that, since allegory was at that time used extensively by Philo in his interpretation of Scripture, Paul is referring to the allegory of Philo. This hardly seems possible since as a technical term for Scripture interpretation allegory was not known during the first century, but became the accepted method used especially by the church fathers of Alexandria. The allegorical interpretation developed by Philo and later adopted by Christian scholars gave free rein to arbitrary exposition of Scripture so that the interpreter could extract whatever he desired from the Bible. The Scripture became a magician's hat out of which the interpreter could pull whatever he had placed in it.

Paul's allegory has more in common with the rabbinic midrashim which he surely knew as a student under Gamaliel. These interpretations of the Scripture in Jewish literature often employ the allegory, as may be seen in the midrash on Genesis 40:9, where the vine in Pharaoh's dream is Israel and the three branches are Moses, Aaron, and Miriam. The Song of Solomon is a description of God and Israel. In Galatians Paul uses allegory much like the midrashim, and it is very similar to the allusions discussed previously. The significant factor to be noted here is that Paul takes hold of historical events which are paralleled with circumstances in the church.

To distinguish typology from allegory we may well quote a definition by Johann Gerhard, a Lutheran theologian of the seventeenth century: It is a type when any Old Testament fact is shown to have been done or yet to be done in the New Testament. It is an allegory when anything of the Old or New Testament is explained with a new sense and is accommodated to a spiritual doctrine or way of life. A type consists in the comparison of facts. An allegory is occupied not so much with facts as with their incidentals from which it draws out useful and hidden doctrines.[8]

Allegory is very much attached to the text, and indeed to the very words and letters from which hidden meanings may be extracted; and it is further characterized by an unbridled freedom in matters of spiritual interpretation. In contrast, typology is remarkably free from attachment to the words or letters of the text, but is bound to a great degree to the historical phenomena of the text. Typology searches for the events in history in which correspondence and similarity can be seen. Allegory, on the other hand, is little concerned with events, for it looks for comparison of ideas and doctrines. It does not ask how an event took place, but what its spiritual meaning is. Typology insists that the events shall determine the meaning which is to be derived from them.

To the above uses of the Old Testament we should add that it was appealed to as authority for life. In refuting a tradition that nullified honor for parents Jesus cited the commandment, "Honor your father and your mother," and he enforced his argument by quoting further from the ancient law, "He who speaks evil of father or mother, let him surely die" (Mt. 15:4). Similarly in the discussion about divorce Jesus quoted a verse from the creation account in the second chapter of Genesis to establish the priority of the permanence of marriage over the permission for divorce (19:3-8). When he was asked how to obtain eternal life, he answered, "If you would enter life, keep the commandments" (19:17). Paul also appeals to the Old

Testament to establish his admonition to overcome evil with good by citing a passage from Proverbs, "if your enemy is hungry, feed him" (Rom. 12:20). It is needless to cite other examples to indicate how readily the Old Testament was used for instruction in holy living. "Whatever was written in former days was written for our instruction, that by steadfastness and by the encouragement of the scriptures we might have hope" (Rom. 15:4).

Since citations and references are numerous—totals vary from 160 to 4150—[9] one may expect to find variations in the methods and the purposes for citing the Old Testament. Our survey intended to stay within modest limits to make soundings which rather accurately reflect the wide area of Old Testament citations. Excellent handbooks on New Testament hermeneutics are at hand for further exploration of this interesting field.[10]

Summary

A few summary statements are appropriate at this point.

1. The New Testament writers appeal to events in the history of Israel to find parallels to the events taking place in the new age which the coming of Christ has introduced. These writers found the events of the exodus out of Egypt and of the restoration out of Babylonian exile particularly fitting. The former, with its deliverance of Israel from bondage to become the people of God, was used in several ways to represent the deliverance of the church from sin and death to become the

21

people of God. The latter, especially since the prophet of the exile (Is. 40-55), described the role of the Servant of the LORD and became the pattern par excellence for the ministry and suffering of Christ and for the mission of the church.

2. The writers of the New Testament were selective in using not only certain events to the neglect of others, but also in their use of details of passages cited. Much like the parables of Jesus in which the main theme is not concerned with the details, so the writers used only those elements of the Old Testament story that established parallels in the New Testament narrative, such as the weeping of Rachel and of the mothers in Bethlehem. We ought not to conclude that only those events or texts that are cited are being fulfilled or have relevance for understanding the new age. Rather we should observe that the principle of selecting parts serves to include the whole, which is to say that the Old Testament as a whole, viewed as the established Word of God, was realizing its fulfillment. Jesus' cry of dereliction from the cross, taken from Psalm 22, could not but make that psalm most beloved for fulfillment citations. Yet the cries of forsakenness in many non-cited psalms, in Job, or in Jeremiah are not thereby excluded from fulfillment. The part incorporates the whole so that we may assume that the entire Old Testament was incorporated in the concept of fulfillment.

3. The methods of the various writers correspond substantially to those in the rabbinic midrashim and to the *pesher* interpretations at Qumran. It would not display a Christian preju-

dice to observe that the New Testament writers are less given to vagaries and arbitrariness than their contemporaries. In our day we have been schooled to find the grammatical interpretation with its historical setting to learn the mind of the author as accurately as possible. Consequently, present-day exegesis may not be too impressed with that of the New Testament. Nor need we be impressed, for the writers did not intend to set up exegetical methods nor did they enjoin us to use their methods. They are asking us to note that they labored with the tools and materials of their time to show that the Old Testament was finding its consummation in the coming of Christ and his church. They were men of their age called to write for the readers of their age.

4. Finally, if we may think of the Old Testament as a tapestry with many loose ends, then the New Testament writers are weavers who select many of the threads to weave them into a newly begun tapestry in which the picture of Christ appears. The Old Testament strands give color, substance, and background to enhance the beauty and the meaning of the Risen Lord. Further, the strands are so thoroughly interwoven into the new fabric that the Old cannot be pulled out of the New. The two have become one flesh, to use another figure. What God has joined together, let not man put asunder.

NOTES

1. Frederic W. Farrar, *History of Interpretation* (London: Macmillan and Co., 1886), pp. 18-22.

2. E. R. Goodenough, "Philo Judeus," *The Interpreter's Dictionary of the Bible*, K-Q (Nashville: Abingdon, 1962), 796-799. For Philo's "Allegorical Interpretation of Genesis II., III." read *Philo*, The Loeb Classical Library (New York: G. P. Putnam's Sons, 1929), I, 140-484.

3. F. F. Bruce, *Biblical Exegesis in the Qumran Texts* (Grand Rapids, Michigan: Wm. B. Eerdmans Publishing Co., 1959).

4. C. H. Dodd, *According to the Scriptures* (London: Nisbet & Co., Ltd., 1952), pp. 28-60. Cf. also a critical survey of the "Testimony Book" hypothesis by E. E. Ellis, *Paul's Use of the Old Testament* (Edinburgh: Oliver and Boyd, 1957), pp. 98-113.

5. Bertil Gärtner makes a good case for the verbal root *natzar*, "keep, preserve," as the background for Nazarene. In Isaiah 49:6 *nᵉtzûrê*, "the preserved ones" (Qere reading), has the restored people of Israel in mind. In Isaiah 42:6 and 49:8, where this verb appears, the Lord has preserved the Servant to be a covenant to the people and a light to the nations. In the account of Jesus' being preserved from the wrath of Herod, Matthew may have seen in Nazareth a fitting allusion to the Hebrew root *natzar*. *Die rätselhaften Termini Nazoräer und Iskariot* (Uppsala: Appelbergs Boktryekere A B, 1957).

6. Dodd, *op. cit.*, pp. 61 ff.

7. W. Eichrodt, "Is Typological Exegesis an Appropriate Method?" *Essays on Old Testament Hermeneutics*, ed. Claus Westermann (Richmond: John Knox Press, 1963), p. 225.

8. Quoted by G. von Rad, "Typological Interpretation of the Old Testament," *Essays on Old Testament Hermeneutics*, p. 21, n. 7.

9. Passages formally cited as listed by H. B. Swete, number 160, *Introduction to the Old Testament in Greek* (Cambridge: University Press, 1900), pp. 382-86. Various totals are given by R. C. Oudersluys, "Old Testament Quotations in the New Testament," *Reformed Review*, Vol. 14 (March, 1961), 1-2.

10. In addition to the writers cited the following are given: F. Johnson, *The Quotations of the New Testament from the Old* (Philadelphia: American Baptist Publication Society, 1896); K. Stendahl, *The School of Matthew* (Uppsala: C. W. K. Gleerup, 1954); D. M. Turpie, *The Old Testament in the New* (London, 1868); C. H. Toy, *Quotations in the New Testament* (New York: Charles Scribner's Sons, 1884); R. V. G. Tasker, *The Old Testament in the New Testament* (Philadelphia: Westminster Press, 1957).

CHAPTER II

THE USE OF THE OLD TESTAMENT IN THE CHURCH

THE MUCH DISCUSSED RELATIONSHIP BETWEEN the Old Testament and New Testament was once defined by the church father St. Augustine as the New Testament being latent in the Old and the Old Testament becoming patent in the New. Apart from the relationship it seeks to define, this statement reflects the church's full acceptance of the Old Testament as part of the inspired canon. Ascribing inspiration to the Old Testament might seem a simple matter of accepting the Bible which Jesus and the apostles regarded as Scripture, but there was in fact an early struggle concerning the place the Old Testament should have in the Christian community.

Foreshadows of that struggle appear in the New Testament itself. At the council of the church in Jerusalem, described in Acts 15, the authority of the Old Testament to require cultic practices was called into question. Should the Old Testament in its entirety be regulative for the Christian community? Even though the church honored the Old Testament as God's Word, yet she declared that parts of that Word were not binding on Christians.

The apostle Paul, a member of that council, later elaborated on this question in his writings to emphasize the point that the Old Testament law in no instance had regulative control; in fact, to insist on the necessity of the law for justification would be to nullify the death of Christ (Gal. 3:21). The writer of the Hebrews described the Old Covenant as obsolete and passing away, which, to say the least, places it on a secondary level. From these and other examples we gather that the church, although she revered the Old Testament, yet assumed the right to set parts of it aside.

Early Church to Augustine

The church's readiness to open the canon to other writings could not but intensify hostility between Christians and Jews. Not only did Christians raise the words of Jesus and the writings of evangelists and apostles to equal rank with the Old Testament, but they also began to give recognition to non-canonical Jewish literature now known as Apocrypha. Because of the bitter enmity that developed, Christians would more and more question the competence of Judaism to determine the limits of the canon which were ostensibly set at the council of Jamnia around the close of the first century. Moreover, Christians claimed special insight given by the Holy Spirit so that they could normally and rightly draw up a "Christian" canon, which they indeed did. This meant that they looked with favor on some non-canonical writings

27

which in the course of time because of constant use were placed within the Old Testament canon.

The freedom to pass judgment on the canon also expressed itself in rejection of the Old Testament as inferior to the New Testament. Marcion, a radical gnostic, taught that the God of the Old Testament was not the God and Father of Jesus Christ. Consequently, he asserted, the Old Testament had no canonical standing. Against Marcion and other gnostics condemned as heretics, the church declared, among other things, that the Old Testament should be retained as part of the inspired literature incorporated within the Christian canon.

The rejection of Marcionism did not, however, dismiss the problem of how to harmonize the Old Testament teachings with those of the New. How should one, for example, who had been taught to overcome evil with good or to pray for his enemies understand God's command to Joshua to exterminate the Canaanites? What must one do with the psalmists' cries or demands for vindication in the light of Paul's teaching that no one is just in the sight of God? Would not a semi-Marcionism placing the Old Testament on a lower level of inspiration, or regarding it as the vestibule to the New Testament, have settled the matter? The early church fathers did not need to resort to such expedients, for they had a ready device in allegory as a method of interpretation to bring the Old Testament in line with the New. Allegory had previously been used by Philo to harmonize the teachings of the Old Testament with Greek philosophy. It became the method of Christian scholars at Alexandria to find New Testament thought in the Old. Allegory removed the offense of the Old Testament so that its place in the canon was fully justified.

The grammatical-historical school at Antioch of Syria arose in sharp contrast to the allegorical school of Alexandria. In the first place this school gave precedence to the Hebrew text rather than to the LXX. From this text these scholars sought to interpret the Old Testament according to the grammatical-historical sense. This method, one can readily surmise, produced an exegesis at wide variance with that of the Alexandrine school whose allegorical method gave little attention to the historical setting and whose Greek text differed extensively from the Hebrew. However, the Antiochene school also confronted the problem of relating the Old Testament to the New. This relationship was established by means of typology, discussed in our previous chapter. The historical persons and events were regarded as types which foreshadowed the messianic times. On the one hand, the type given in the Old Testament had its historical quality and possessed meaning for its time. Since, however, the Old Testament looked forward for fulfillment of promise, the historical type was the model or picture of the event that brought on fulfillment. The "historical" sense would be considered the lower and the "typical" sense the higher.

Although we are usually interested in assessing the merits of one school in comparison with the other, our interest in these schools at this moment is to point out that they both kept the two Testaments together by means of their exegesis. Perhaps it would be more correct to observe that because of their assumption that the two Testaments were parts of one Book these early fathers were constrained to find some method of interpretation to support that unity. The New Testament indeed urged believers to accept the Old Testament as the Word of God, yet gave no definitive instructions by what means of interpretation the bond between the Old and the New was to be preserved. To be sure, Antioch could appeal to Paul who twice mentioned "types" (Rom. 5:14; I Cor. 10:6), or to the writer of the Hebrews who used typology to designate the heavenly model of the tabernacle in the wilderness (Heb. 8:5). Alexandria in turn could appeal to Paul's use of the term "allegory," if not to his method of using it (Gal. 4:24). Each system ostensibly had New Testament warrant, and each seemed to enhance the unity of the two Testaments.

The traditions of Antioch and Alexandria converge upon the era of the two Latin fathers, Augustine and Jerome, the era which in effect set the pattern for medieval hermeneutics. Since Augustine knew little Hebrew, he was limited to the use of the LXX and consequently regarded it as the inspired text. This text carried the traditions and background of the Alexandrine school. Consequently we are not surprised that allegory played an important role in Augustine's exegesis. His contemporary Jerome, however, because of his scholarly pursuits was influenced by Antioch. Jerome's fame arose primarily from his translating the entire Bible into the vernacular Latin which bears the name Vulgate. This translation was especially praiseworthy because it was taken from the Hebrew text of the Old Testament. Prior to this the Old Latin versions were derived from the LXX text. Jerome's studies took him into Syria where he learned Hebrew and where he gained firsthand knowledge of Antiochene typology. It is not without significance that in spite of the heresies of monophysitism and pelagianism for which Antiochene scholars were condemned by the fifth ecumenical council, Jerome could wholeheartedly prefer the Hebrew test to that of the LXX, and could also accept typology as a hermeneutical principle. "Guilt by association" apparently did not blind him to merits in heterodoxy. Junilius Africanus, bishop of Africa, later became an able representative of Antiochene theology, which he learned in his studies in Persia.

From the time of Augustine to the Reformation exegetical methods were uncritically adopted and used much as they were established by the Latin fathers. Both typology and allegory were in vogue. The four-fold sense of Scripture, a heritage stemming from the Alexandrine fathers, labored the text for its literal sense, then its historical through its allegorical to arrive at its mystical sense. Thus understood the Bible was given to the Germanic peoples of Europe who were won to the Christian church. It would have been unthinkable for these untutored pagan tribes to call the exegesis of their mother church into question. They came as kindergarten pupils into the school of the church whose teachings were accepted without challenge. In this setting the Old Testament served a useful purpose to bring these converts out of their polytheism into true monotheism. Here they learned that there was but one true God who revealed himself to Israel and that worship of other gods was abhorrent in his sight.

The tradition which the church produced through the decrees and dogmas of the councils became an important factor in the interpretation of Scripture. Ideally, tradition was to be equal with the Bible for determining the faith and life of the church. Practically, however, tradition had undesignedly taken up within itself methods for interpreting the Scripture which virtually reduced Scripture to a servant of tradition, a phenomenon which later also plagued Protestantism. If biblical exegesis was fully regulated by the church, there would be no occasion for the problem of the Old Testament to emerge. The problem lay peacefully dormant until the Reformation made the Scripture the only source of authority.

Reformation Age

The coming of the Reformation, however its rise may be attributed to causes outside the church, drove the church to examine the structure of her authority. Since the claim for her authority was derived from Scripture, especially the words of Jesus to the apostle Peter, it became more and more urgent to determine whether the Scriptures were properly understood and interpreted. Had the popes and councils actually been in dialogue with the Word of God, or had they merely indulged in a soliloquy to produce a monolithic structure which, like the Chaldeans described by Habakkuk (1:7), proceeded from itself? Within the church, men who enjoyed the advantages of learning carefully and critically probed the use made of Scripture. It became apparent that Scripture and tradition were caught within a vicious circle in which interpretation produced tradition and tradition in turn controlled interpretation. The circle was broken open as methods of interpretation were called into question because they produced results sought to enhance the dogma and authority of the church. With the breaking of this circle Scripture was released from the hold of tradition and underwent a new reading and interpretation by any who chose to do so.

With this new freedom for studying the Bible two well-known problems appeared again: the problem of hermeneutics and the problem of the relationship of the Old Testament to the New. These interrelated problems were as old as the New Testament itself, but they had engaged the mind of the early church and had ostensibly been solved. Now the Reformation scholars, spurred on by a newly acquired freedom and not yet restrained by later confessional statements, seized the opportunity to let the Scripture be heard as it intended to be heard.[1]

Luther, as the Reformation's foremost spokesman, held that the Scripture was the only source of authority. Councils and dogmas were to be accepted only to the degree that they were in accord with Holy Writ. Although Luther at first used the four-fold method of medieval exegesis he soon abandoned it to find the literal and the spiritual sense of the text. He rejected the use of allegory except in preaching about the cultic laws in Leviticus. The law of the Old Testament had its literal sense but also a spiritual meaning which awakened guilt within man. The words of Scripture were more than mere letters arranged on the page, for these words had spiritual power to bring man to salvation. Thus it was not enough to be satisfied with the literal sense, for the Word was to be encountered in its spiritual power.

The relationship between the Old and New Testament can on the one hand be seen as a contrast between law and gospel, between works and grace, between Moses and Christ, and on the other hand as a unity bound together in Christ who speaks through David and the prophets and appears as the Word made flesh in the New Testament. We do Luther no disservice to describe his perception of the relationship between the Old and New Testaments as a paradox involving contrast and continuity. The contrast takes into account the superiority of the New Testament, and the continuity gives recognition to the presence of the gospel throughout the entire Scripture.

Calvin, in common with other Reformers, recognized the Scriptures as the sole authority for the Christian church. His exegesis may be described as thoroughly grammatical and historical to the extent that was possible in his day. To his exegesis he added practical observations for faith and life. Calvin did not resort to the four-fold sense of Scripture so common among the medieval scholastics. Allegory had no place in his method, but he freely used typology to show the Old Testament promise realized its fulfillment in the New. The relationship between the Testaments appeared in the glory of God revealed to Israel and made manifest when the Word became flesh. Further, the kingdom of God established in the Old Testament found its consummation in the church of the New. The covenant also played an important role in bridging the distance between the two parts of Scripture. Perhaps Calvin's unique emphasis on God's sovereign grace manifested in choosing his people from the beginning of time overarched all the biblical descriptions that united the Old with the New.

Zwingli, who enjoyed a rich training in Greek and Roman thought, embraced a broad view of revelation that esteemed sayings of Plato and Seneca as work of the same Holy Spirit that inspired the biblical writers. The Scripture, however, was inspired throughout, even though within it Zwingli detected laws and customs that had meaning and authority only for Israel. When such portions of the Scripture were properly recognized and discounted, the Scripture became authoritative for the Christian. In his contention with the Anabaptists who sought to build the Christian ethic on the Sermon on the Mount and rejected the Old Testament law as being given only to the Jews, the Swiss Reformer insisted that since God had established one covenant for one people it followed that the Old Testament was also meant for Christians. He did, however, set the Old Testament at a lower level because of its ritual and ceremonies and because of the nationalism which stood in sharp contrast to the open universalism of the New Testament. Differences of rank did indeed exist, but after making due allowance for these limitations Zwingli regarded it unnecessary to remove the Old Testament from the sacred canon.

Any student of Reformation history can readily discern how it came to enrich the life and faith of the Christian church. Importantly, it opened the Bible to be read and interpreted by king and peasant alike. The ecclesiastical stranglehold over reading and interpreting the Scriptures was broken. The Book was liberated from Latin—the language of scholars—and released into the languages of all peoples. In the ecstasy of appreciation for the newly uncovered treasure we rarely see any mention of the problems that the "open" Bible brought with it. The happy privilege of a free and unfettered use of the Scriptures all but blots out the thought of any problem. Even today the many Bible Societies established for translating and distributing the Bible throughout the world embody the same Reformation ideal that all mankind should possess it as an "open" book to be read and interpreted according to the readers' insights. However, no attention is given to the problems of interpretation and of Old and New Testament relationship. This cautionary comment does not imply that the gain of an "open" Bible has been nullified by the problems thereby projected. Quite the contrary! The point is rather that these problems are not readily observed and that they emerge especially when confessional statements are made or when preaching and teaching the Bible must come to grips with these difficulties.

As suggested above, the Reformers were agreed in ascribing primary authority to the Scripture. Further, the canon of the Old and the New Testaments was retained even though all books were not accorded equal veneration. In no instance was it deemed necessary to remove any book from the canon. The main point of difficulty concerned the place the Old Testament should have in the life and faith of the Christian church. Luther's position primarily established a contrast between the Old and New as between law and gospel. To be sure, he found Christ in many parts of the Old Testament, and asserted that Christ bound the Old with the New. Calvin labored to confirm the unity of the Bible in accord with his presupposition that one God had ordained one redemption for one people. Zwingli held the Old Testament rather loosely, especially at those parts which fell below the spiritual tone of the New. In effect, the Reformers worked around a paradox which may be stated as follows: The Old Testament is part of the sacred canon and therefore authoritative, but it has secondary status in that it serves as preparation for the New.

The above paradox, issuing directly from the

Scripture itself, had remained quiet under the spell of ecclesiastical authority. The spell was broken; the paradox became alive. The Reformers initiated the effort to resolve the tension of the paradox.

Post-Reformation Period

As Protestantism became more and more established it needed less defense against the Roman Church. Its authority was now vested in the Bible, which became the object of study and evaluation. In its most conservative declaration, the Formula Consensus of the Second Helvetic Confession (1675), reformed theologians of Switzerland declared that the words, the letters, the vowel points, and punctuation were given under the direction of the Holy Spirit, and therefore all were inspired. Comparisons of the Hebrew text with then-known versions and variations within manuscripts revealed that the Consensus was an overstatement, for vowels were a later addition to the Hebrew text and scribal changes in the transmission of the text could be discerned. The text which had been accepted as the Word of God contained evidence of human attempts to make that Word more readable and understandable. The human-temporal element in fact played an important role in the transmission of the Scriptures.

Significant contributions of post-Reformation biblical research for interpretation of the Old Testament involve literary and historical criticism. Since the word "criticism" lends itself to an erroneous interpretation we should bear in mind the two usages of that word: fault-finding or passing severe judgment, and investigation or research. We refer here to the latter definition. By the eighteenth century methods and principles of criticism were in common use in studies of classical literature and of Semitic writings which were coming into the hands of European scholars. From Jean Astruc's publication of his Memoirs in 1753, in which he detected two literary sources for the book of Genesis, until our day, literary analysis of books of the Bible has engaged many scholars in determining the sources and times of writing of parts of Scripture. Long held views such as that Moses was the writer of the Pentateuch, Isaiah the author of the sixty-six chapters in his book, and Paul the author of Hebrews were challenged and declared to be untenable in the light of the evidence from the Bible. Furthermore, in line with the prevailing Hegelian notions of progress and development, writings were assigned dates according to a sequence of lower to higher levels of thought. Even though variations and disagreements, not to mention rejections of conclusions, appeared among scholars, a general consensus concerning literary sources and times of writing developed. Because of phenomenal archaeological discoveries in the Near East during the past fifty to seventy-five years, conclusions in biblical criticism have been and are being revised. These discoveries have produced volumes of literature concerning ancient worship, law, wisdom, and history, so that literary and historical criticism will continue to be an interesting and profitable discipline in biblical studies.

The church, both Protestant and Roman Catholic, at first reacted unfavorably toward the results of criticism. The issue in conflict was the divine quality of the Bible. Some questioned the propriety, if not the rightness, of subjecting the Holy Book to methods of analysis used for secular writings. Others were loathe to acknowledge any human or fallible elements within the sacred writings. Moreover, many scholars carried on biblical research with no indication that they accepted the Old Testament as the revelation of God. If the ancient writers were simply producing from their situation in life literature about God, man, and the world, then the Bible can and does become a history of the religion of Israel. However, if some scholars indeed regarded the Old Testament as merely the text of the religion or history of Israel, others found that the results of criticism enhanced their understanding of the revelation of God given to Israel through her history. Furthermore, since the Old Testament intends to show that God's redemption took place in the course of history, it became especially important to know the historical context in which God revealed himself. Thus, it became increasingly clear that biblical research could be indispensable for understanding the Bible. As a result we can discern a steady trend among Protestant and Roman Catholic scholars to accept the results of biblical criticism. We refer to this change as a trend to imply that a sizeable portion of churches and scholars react unfavorably, even as churches did in the past.[2]

Since the Old Testament reflects the moral

and religious standard of Israel's day, a standard not totally similar to that of the teachings of Jesus and the apostles, it was not surprising for church-men of post-Reformation times to give it less than unqualified approval. The various branches of the Protestant church acknowledged the divine character of the Book and that it served as the historical introduction to the New Testament. However, it could not be used to establish Christian doctrine unless it had been reinterpreted in the light of the New Testament. Cries for vengeance and the principle of retribution were not in conformity with the New Testament's injunction to love one's enemy. Some regarded the Old Testament as an elementary school book which had value for instructing the Jews, but obviously no longer had that value for Christians. The theologian Schleier-macher made no distinction between the Old Testament and pagan literature, for both, he asserted, could equally serve as an introduction to the New Testament. Judaism had an advantage over pagan faiths in that it was in historical line with Christianity, and it would therefore seem reasonable to retain the Old Testament for the sake of historical continuity and enrichment, but it would be erroneous to use it as the foundation for the Christian faith. Many could agree to the use of the prophets and psalms for high moral teachings and for use in worship; but this partial acceptance was not an endorsement of the entire Old Testament.

Scholars such as G. F. Oehler and L. Diestel placed the Old Testament in the progressive revelation of God. They suggested that it be read in

41

the setting of Israel's life where the process of revelation began. This implied a difference in levels of ethical and religious thought between the two Testaments, and this meant that Christians should not appeal indiscriminately to the Old Testament for instruction in faith and life. In warning against using the Old Testament as a repository for Christian doctrine, Diestel advised that the historical setting of the Old Testament be taken into account, that the development of religious thought be observed, and that the Old Testament, related to and interpreted by the New Testament, could be used profitably in the thought and life of the Christian church. Thus he related the Old Testament to the Christian faith.

Since through her history the Christian church gave priority to the New Testament, it is noteworthy to observe a few instances in which the Old Testament laws and customs were embraced for regulation of life. During their brief history the Münsterites, a branch of the Anabaptist movement, modelled their community after the kingdom of Israel. Practices such as polygamy, circumcision, and observing the Old Testament dietary laws were part of the community's life at the cost of its being held in disrepute. In England the dissenters found that the prophets were most useful instruments for denouncing the oppressive rule of kings and priests. Sabbath legislation became especially strong through the influence of the Puritans on civic life, and certain "fringe" groups observed the Old Testament laws of circumcision and diet. More recently Seventh Day Adventism

42

has carried on these observances. The law of the tithe found, and still finds, much acceptance, especially because of its practicality for the support of church work. The above survey, to which the observance of marriage laws and of not taking interest on loans may be added, indicates how little the customs and laws of the Old Testament served to regulate the life of the church.

In summary, the Reformation church was disposed to keep the Old Testament as part of the sacred canon. She was disposed to use it as the fitting and enlightening historical introduction to the New Testament. If we have rightly heard the servants of this church, in her more circumspect acceptance of the Old Testament, she has made sure that the Old Testament Word be evaluated, corrected, and completed by the New Testament Word; and in her less discerning moments has indiscriminately made the Old Testament serve her doctrinal statement or way of life. Her labors have been both her burden and her joy. Much like a composer of a symphony after laboring with his theme through different movements may find no solution for his theme, but in the searching produces the beauty and ecstasy of the symphony, so have the labors of the church produced no solution, but while she labors she hears the symphony of God's redemption for the world issue forth from both the Old and New Testaments.

The Problem Today

Our final purpose in this chapter is to view

the main lines of thought on our subject as expressed by scholars of the past half century. Lest any reader should entertain hopes of a new solution to an old problem, he should be properly forewarned by the words of the Preacher "That which is, already has been; that which is to be, already has been" (Eccles. 3:15). A better maxim for our purpose, however, is to be found in the paradox: History never repeats itself, and history always repeats itself.

The results of recent discussions concerning the Old-New Testament relationship may be summarized under three heads:

1. The low point of view which would dismiss the Old Testament from the sacred canon.

2. The high point of view which regards the Old Testament as the primary source of revelation.

3. The moderate point of view which sublimates the Old Testament to the New but retains it as part of divine revelation.

1. The low point of view. We may recall that during the second century Marcion reacted radically against the Old Testament to exclude it from the canon. He affirmed that the God of the Old Testament was not the God and Father of Jesus Christ. In his work on Marcion the renowned historian Harnack claimed that the ancient heretic was right in his judgment of the Old Testament. He regretted that the Reformers had not gone further and placed the Old Testament books in the same category as the Apocrypha. Much of the opposition to Christianity, so Harnack alleged, stems from the offense arising out of the Old Testament.

44

Even though Jesus regarded it as Scripture, we need not do so since Jesus himself affirmed that all true knowledge of God comes through him (Mt. 11:17). Harnack did not press his point as did Friedrich Delitzsch, the famous Old Testament scholar, who in his two-volume work *Die grosse Täuschung* (1920-21) went to great lengths to point out the inferior quality of the Old Testament in the light of the New, and consequently urged that the Old Testament be removed from the canon, in order to enhance the witness of the church.

More recently E. Hirsch in his *Das Alte Testament und die Predigt des Evangeliums* (1936) contended that the Old Testament serves as the antithesis to the Christian faith based on the New Testament. He was especially influenced by Kierkegaard, who regarded the Old Testament as the negative background by which the excellence of the New Testament becomes clear. Hirsch tolerated the Old Testament only as the antithesis to the New. He lived during the fierce anti-Semitic outrage in Germany and this may have in part induced him to relieve the church of the Old Testament burden as he saw it. But his devaluation of the Old Testament was too one-sided and arbitrary, for the Old Testament includes teachings concerning faith and conduct that are not antithetical to the New, but stand in close harmony with it.

The low view receives very thorough exposition by R. Bultmann in his essays "The Significance of the Old Testament for the Christian Faith"[3] and "Prophecy and Fulfillment."[4]

In the first essay Bultmann declares that regarding Jesus as a continuation of the Old Testament prophets' emphasis upon the true worship of God and outgoing love for one's neighbor has robbed the New Testament of its uniqueness and has made it a refined Judaism. If, however, embracing the Christian faith one recognizes Jesus Christ as the unique revelation of God, then the Old Testament can have no validity in matters of faith.

The particular purpose of the Old Testament is to give man understanding of his existence as sinner under the demands of the law. However, the Gentile apart from the Old Testament also stands as sinner under the demands of the law of conscience. We who have been under the Old and New Testament influence do not readily appreciate that the demands of the law that drive the sinner in his guilt to Jesus Christ for pardon do exist apart from the Old Testament as Paul asserted (Rom. 1:32; 2:14-16). Hence Bultmann argues that merely because the Old Testament awakens man to a sense of sin and guilt does not mean it is the unique Word of God.

Bultmann correctly observes that within the Old Testament we have both law and gospel, guilt and forgiveness. These are fully communicated by God to Israel in her history. Although God's forgiving grace does not appear on every page of the Old Testament, yet an impressive portion witnesses to God's faithful grace to his wayward people. It must be noted that this grace was mediated to Israel as a people. The call of Abraham, the deliverance from Egypt, and the restoration from Babylon are favors bestowed on Israel, not on those outside that nation.

In contrast to the above the final act of God's grace in Jesus Christ is not restricted to a people within one historical process. Israel's history does not parallel the history of the Christian community which comes from many ethnic backgrounds. Since this act of God in Christ takes on worldwide dimensions, the Christian church has no significant tie with the Old Testament redemptive history. Therefore the Old Testament is no longer a revelation for the Christian as it has been and still is for the Jew.

The Old Testament serves a useful purpose for helping the Christian understand the claims of God upon man, hear the demands of the law, and realize the forgiveness of God's grace. It is here that the Christian can see himself mirrored as a sinner being reconciled to God in Christ. This then would make the Old Testament Word an indirect Word of God for the Christian. The Christian may take hold of the Old Testament which was spoken as God's Word for another situation in order to prepare him for hearing the Word of Christ spoken in the present situation. In this sense, Bultmann asserts, the Old Testament may be called prophecy which is fulfilled in the New Testament.

In the second essay, "Prophecy and Fulfillment," Bultmann takes hold of three concepts that sought fulfillment: the covenant, the kingdom, and the people. Each of these concepts represented God's relationship to Israel, and each failed to

47

reach fulfillment. The covenant to be fulfilled in Israel's history required cultic ceremonies which ignored moral demands. Since Israel was unable to meet the moral requirements of God's law and relied on cultic ceremonies, the covenant of the Old Testament miscarried. The concept of kingdom which extols God as King identified this rule of God with historical Israel. However, especially after the Babylonian exile, the idea of the kingdom being embodied by historical Israel as a world power became less likely, and realization was sought in some eschatological hope. The concept of kingdom miscarried here also.

The miscarriage of the concepts of covenant, kingdom, and people which is seen in the Old Testament turns out to be the negative side of promise which looks forward to fulfillment. Fulfillment was finally realized in the coming of Jesus Christ, for in him God has changed the failure of the Old Testament into an achieved reality. This reality has a two-fold dimension in that the kingdom and people are within the here-and-now of secular history and are oriented toward the full reality of the return of Jesus Christ. The point is that the miscarriage of the Old Testament issues into the promise which finds fulfillment in Jesus Christ.

2. The high point of view for the Old Testament is most ably presented by A. A. van Ruler of Utrecht University in *Die Christliche Kirche und das Alte Testament*.[5] Van Ruler is much impressed with God's deep concern for the world which he created and for the practical daily affairs of Israel's

life. This kind of impression must be seen in contrast to the New Testament's spiritual teachings concerning guilt and forgiveness in man's relationship to God through Jesus Christ. Van Ruler takes hold of the theme of the kingdom of God as the primary witness of the Old Testament. This kingdom is the Old Testament's "plus" over against the New.[6] The "plus" of the New Testament over against the Old, in turn, is the deity of Jesus. This "plus" of the Old Testament, the theocracy, deals with the common affairs of life, such as the possession of the land, the social and economic life, the administration of justice, and the development of culture. These are the "politics" of God in the widest and best sense of that word.[7] To put this in a phrase, it is the sanctification of the earth.

It is van Ruler's contention that in her preaching the Christian church needs to present not only the doctrine of Jesus Christ, but more especially the kingdom of God which Jesus Christ came to establish. That kind of preaching will come to grips with the earthly matters about which the Old Testament speaks. If the preaching of the church is largely restricted to the New Testament, then the spiritualizing of earthly matters takes place with the result that the church becomes unrelated to the world. Since the Old Testament may be considered God's first approach to the world, the church should carefully observe that that approach revolved about the day-by-day this-world existence of the people that God had redeemed. The rule of God, the theocracy, was not an eschatological prospect as commonly envisaged by

49

Christians who rely heavily on the New Testament. It was rather the a priori motif that was being expressed throughout the Old Testament. The New Testament filled in that basic pattern through the forgiveness and reconciliation of Christ. The Old Testament then is more than a convenient and perhaps necessary background for understanding the New Testament message; and surely it is more than a recital of dead legalism or a miscarriage of the Old Testament covenant and ideal.

3. The moderate point of view. This point of view will mediate between the first two. To mediate between different positions on any matter implies both a partial acceptance and a partial rejection in hopes of finding a middle way which embodies a synthesis of all the important positive factors in the two positions.

Any evaluation of scholars such as Harnack and Hirsch in their low views of the Old Testament must recognize that they have indeed uncovered certain "low" levels in the record of Israel's history. Difficult as it is for those of us who have grown up in a tradition that makes the entire Old Testament the authoritative Word of God to see something inferior in it, we ought not let a tradition blind us and keep us from seeing the Old Testament as it really is. We ought to recognize that these scholars have pointed out some serious faults in the Old Testament's witness—the narratives of vengeance and guile, the extermination of pagan nations, or the laws for the execution of heretics. One who has embraced the Gospel of love and forgiveness cannot but be embarrassed with the sub-Christian, if not non-Christian, parts of the Old Testament.

We are not the first to have seen these parts of the Scripture. Throughout her history the church knew these parts as well as we. Yet she was not minded to regard the Old Testament as non-canonical or a less sacred part of the Bible, for she listened to some parts of the Old Testament with as much profit as to the New. She heard the Word of God through prophets and psalmists as clearly as through apostles and evangelists. Through the lens of the New Testament the church focused her attention on the Old and accepted it as the proper preparation for the coming of Christ the LORD. So it was that the church adopted the Old Testament as a whole, fully cognizant that she could not use it all as normative for the faith and life which the Spirit had given to the new creation of God. Within that Old Testament the church found proper attitudes of contrition and humility before God; she observed God's redeeming grace for his wayward people; and she learned the principles for the establishing of God's rule upon earth. These were some of the postive values that the church saw in the Old Testament.

But the church, especially since Reformation times, has seen some negative features in the Old Testament. In his essay "The Hermeneutical Problem of the Old Testament," F. Baumgartel selects as typical instances such shortcomings as the sinister and murderous deeds of Jehu and the demand for vindication in Psalm 26.[8] When we confront shortcomings of this nature we ought, with as much integrity as we possess, to admit that these are low levels in the sacred canon which clearly indicate that God came to Israel, or rather to man, where man actually lived and thought. God's redemptive act and word occurred there. It must then be understood that such acts and words are below the level of the New Testament acts and words, and therefore are not normative or authoritative for Christians.

The position of van Ruler, as described above, may be seen as a vigorous protest, on the one hand, against those who dismiss the Old Testament as of little value for the Christian church and, on the other hand, against those who read a New Testament interpretation into the Old Testament, a somewhat ingenious Christologizing to remove the offense. Let it be said with hearty appreciation that van Ruler has defended the Old Testament against the low judgments passed upon it and has delivered it from the sentimentalization of those who fail to see any problems in it. We may well heed van Ruler's emphasis that in the Old Testament God encounters man in his total need, a need which involves his earthly existence.

After acknowledging our debt to van Ruler for his imaginative and valuable insight, we still are not convinced that he has taken into account all the data of both the Old and New Testaments. The kingdom of God as seen in Israel also appears in the church of the New Testament, and indeed in the church's earthly existence to which the epistles especially attest. The New Testament contains more than teachings about a spiritual relationship with God through Jesus Christ, for it instructs the church how to conduct herself in the daily struggle with the forces of the world in which she actually lived. Moreover, the Old Testament is more than the record of the theocracy in its encounter with human needs and problems. It also describes problems of anxiety and despair that disrupt the believer's personal and spiritual relationship with God. Further, psalmists and prophets deal with subjects such as penitence, forgiveness, and joy, all elements that describe spiritual and individual relationships.

In compressing the data of the Old Testament within the concept of theocracy van Ruler has not determined what the "low levels" of theocracy, such as the institution of slavery, the regulations for marriage, the cancelation of debts, only to mention a few of the laws of the theocracy, should mean for the Christian church. His book gives the impression that once the Old Testament is seen as God's kingdom coming into the world, the problem of preaching that kingdom will not arise. We must surely admit that the principles of that kingdom have reached new and higher dimensions, even this-worldly dimensions, in the New Testament. In what way, one is moved to ask, can we now make use of the pattern of the Old Testament kingdom which in the language of the New· is declared to be old and obsolete?

Since van Ruler has recovered a much needed emphasis in the understanding and presentation of the Old Testament, we are loathe to be critical of his work. However, his point of view indulges an arbitrary selection of data that unfortunately fails to do justice to both Old and New Testaments.[9]

Proposed Solution

The study pursued in this chapter will have achieved its purpose if it has made clear that the Christian church, through its various spokesmen, acknowledged both Testaments as the Word of God. This study has also observed that the church struggled with the difficult problem of how she should use the Old Testament in an age far removed from the conditions of life in ancient Israel. Impossible as it has been to find a method to satisfy all minds, each generation and each branch of Christendom have attempted to find a method which would make the Old Testament a living Word for the new age. Lest we let the problem go by ignoring it, and lest we handle it carelessly or capriciously, we ought to establish a workable method that will do justice to the full counsel of God as it issues from both parts of Scripture.

1. The historical event must be clearly understood. During the past few decades biblical scholarship has discerned that the Old Testament revelation is presented through the mighty acts of God in history. It is therefore necessary for the interpreter to know the historical background and furthermore to comprehend the author's interpretation of the event he narrates. A careful and patient reading of the entire account will disclose what the author intends his readers or listeners to learn about the acts of God. Let us cite a case in

54

point. The historian of Judges has declared his purpose for writing in 2:11-23. The history of the Judges was cast into the cycle of apostasy, judgment, deliverance, and rest. The details of the exploits of the judges are presented to serve the main theme of God's judgment on Israel's rebellion and the compassion which moved him to redeem his people. The author apparently feared that readers would become enamored with details as in the case of Samson, and he expressly warned against a departure from the theme of the book (cf. 14:1-4).

Since books like Psalms and the Wisdom Literature do not readily present a historical setting, it becomes difficult if not impossible to determine a historical background. Here, of necessity, we must resort to surmise and conjecture and probe the known history of Israel to find an appropriate setting. Since the major part of the Old Testament presents its witness in the context of historical events, it would be reasonable to assume that poets and wisemen wrote from the context of event, rather than from philosophical speculation.

2. The Old Testament event embodies promise for the future. The promise received a partial fulfillment within the scope of Israel's life, yet is more elaborate and varied than envisaged by those receiving the promise. In the nation's prosperity historians recalled the fulfillment of the redemptive acts of God begun in Israel's infancy, and in the nation's dark night of exile the prophet arose to speak because he had seen the light of fulfillment which God would bring to pass, a fulfillment surely never imagined by those who in

55

previous generations had experienced the redeeming favor of God. Thus it was also when apostles and evangelists saw fulfillment in the magnitude and universality of believers within the church.

Fulfillment realized in part within Israel's history, and fulfillment breaking forth into new dimensions in the New Testament, is the theme that properly conditions our mind in our use of the Old Testament. From this source we follow the wondrous trail of redemptive fulfillment that reaches new heights in every succeeding age of the church.

3. The Old Testament is to be related to the New. Since we have accepted the New as the fulfillment of the Old Testament promise and hope, in our use of the Old Testament we are compelled to find correspondence, enlargement, and realization in the New. To present the Old in isolation from the New is to run the risk of offering a truncated understanding of the faith. Lest any inferior portion of the Old should control the preaching of the church, it is necessary that every Old Testament passage should be brought under the light of the New for correction, improvement, and enlargement, so that the full understanding of the faith may not be hindered. We have been forewarned in the temptation of Jesus that an appeal to the Old Testament may serve an evil purpose. To avoid any well-meaning but erroneous use of the Old Testament we would be well advised to relate the Old Testament to the New.

4. The redemptive acts of God must be represented. Martin Noth in his discerning essay

"The 'Re-presentation' of the Old Testament in Proclamation" points out that Israel was constantly re-presenting the saving acts of God through her feasts.[10] It was at times such as the observance of the Passover that Israel relived the deliverance from Egypt. The purpose was not merely to relive an ancient event, but to have something like a recurrence of deliverance take place in the present life.

We may well take the narrative of ancient Israel's redemptive history, and re-present it as fully consummated in the redemptive act of Christ. Further, that redemptive history should be re-presented so that it has meaning for every generation in the life of the church. It would then become the privilege of the church to recall the redemptive acts begun in Israel and fulfilled in Jesus Christ; and each generation would realize at least a partial consummation in its ongoing life, and would await the final consummation at the appearing of our LORD.

NOTES

1. E. G. Kraeling, *The Old Testament Since the Reformation* (New York: Harper & Brothers, 1955). This book gives an excellent survey of the Old Testament problem from Reformation times to the present.

2. For an informative and well-documented work on the church's initial reaction against, and later acceptance of, biblical criticism read W. B. Glover, *Evangeli-*

cal Nonconformists and Higher Criticism in the Nineteenth Century (London: Independent Press Ltd., 1954).

3. R. Bultmann, "The Significance of the Old Testament for the Christian Faith," *The Old Testament and Christian Faith*, ed. B. W. Anderson (New York: Harper & Row, 1963), pp. 8-35.

4. R. Bultmann, "Prophecy and Fulfillment," *Essays on Old Testament Hermeneutics*, ed. Claus Westermann (Richmond: John Knox Press, 1963), pp. 50-75.

5. A. A. van Ruler, *Die Christliche Kirche und das Alte Testament* (München: Chr. Kaiser Verlag, 1955). English Translation, *The Christian Church and the Old Testament* (Grand Rapids: Eerdmans Publishing Co., 1971).

6. *Ibid.*, p. 71 (ET p. 77).

7. *Ibid.*, p. 85 (ET p. 91).

8. F. Baumgartel, "The Hermeneutical Problem of the Old Testament," *Essays on Old Testament Hermeneutics*, pp. 134-59.

9. Critical reviews of van Ruler's book appear in *Essays on Old Testament Hermeneutics*. See J. J. Stamm, "Jesus Christ and the Old Testament," pp. 200-10, and Th. C. Vriezen, "Theocracy and Soteriology," pp. 211-23.

10. Martin Noth, "The 'Re-presentation' of the Old Testament in Proclamation," *Essays on Old Testament Hermeneutics*, pp. 76-88.

CHAPTER III

COVENANT AND HISTORY

THE RELATIONSHIP BETWEEN GOD AND ISRAEL was often expressed in terms of covenant, a concept of relationship common in the ancient world. Studies by Mendenhall show that covenants were used in the old city state of Sumer in the third millennium B.C. Their use continued in Assyrian and Hittite nations in the next millennium. The Hittite covenants, many of which still survive, were of two kinds, the suzerainty covenant and the parity covenant. The former was given by a superior, usually a ruler, to an inferior who pledged with an oath to show loyalty to his lord for benefits he had received. The parity covenant was an agreement between equals, such as the Hittite-Egyptian covenant of Ramesis II drawn up at the time of the Exodus.[1]

The suzerainty covenant began with a prologue in which the sovereign told of his benevolence toward his subjects which placed them under obligation to give unqualified allegiance to their lord. A copy of the covenant was deposited in the temple and it was to be read periodically to remind the subjects of their duty toward their king. The gods of the ruler and of the ruled people were called to witness the solemn covenant. Blessings would follow obedience to the terms of the covenant and curses were pronounced over breaking the agreement.

In the Mosaic covenant (Ex. 19) we can discern interesting parallels in that the gracious favor of the LORD has been demonstrated to Israel (ver. 4), and that Israel is to obey the voice of the LORD (ver. 5). As reward for obedience Israel would be a special people of God to be known as "a kingdom of priests and a holy nation" (ver. 6). In the Exodus account of the covenant there is no listing of blessings and curses but this does appear in Deuteronomy, and no witnesses are mentioned, for there is no witness higher than God who established the covenant. Consequently we may observe interesting similarities and differences between the covenant structures of the Old Testament and surrounding nations.

The Hebrew word *berîth,* "covenant," is of uncertain derivation. It occurs most frequently with the verb *karath,* "cut," which may refer to the ceremony of cutting in two the sacrificial victim at the celebration of drawing up the covenant (Jer. 34:18, **cf.** also Gen. 15:7-21). Other verbs used with *berîth* are *nathan,* "give, set," *qûm* in hiphil, "raise up, establish." Verbs that indicate that the covenant has been broken are *'abhar,* "transgress," *parar,* "break," *ma'as,* "despise," *'azabh,* "forsake," and *shakhah,* "forget." The covenant at Sinai was basically the decalogue which became known as the book of the covenant (Ex. 24:7; Deut. 4:13; II Kings 23:2). In a broader sense the covenant incorporated the *huqqim*, "statutes," the *mitzwoth*, "commandments," and the *mishpatim*, "ordinances" (Deut. 4:14, 40; 26:17).

The Sinaitic covenant, given at the time Israel became a nation, placed Israel under obligation to keep the covenant by obeying the law. At the solemn ratification of the covenant Moses rehearsed all the requirements of the LORD[2] to which Israel responded, "all that the LORD has spoken we will do, and we will be obedient" (Ex. 24:7). The covenant code (Ex. 21-23), which follows the decalogue, spelled out the requirements which Israel would keep and observe. However, early in Israel's life it became apparent that she was not able to keep the covenant as the worship of the golden calf at Mt. Sinai illustrated dramatically. Thus, at the beginning of Israel's history and throughout that history, the problem of a violated or broken covenant emerged as an important factor in the God-Israel relationship. The issue which the golden calf incident raised can be phrased in terms of the question whether the covenant stands or falls because of Israel's obedience or disobedience. Surely we should not entertain any suggestion that God was under an illusion about Israel's ability to keep the covenant. We are closer to an understanding of this issue if we regard the keeping of the covenant as an open possibility in which God related himself to Israel. Perhaps the issue should be cast into another form by asking whether, in spite of Israel's disobedience or even her obedience, the covenantal relationship continued so that thereby God's unmerited favor for his people might repeatedly be manifested. In spite of Israel's faithlessness, God remained faithful so that the covenant instituted by God continued in effect. Thus, at the very outset, the problem of the broken covenant was solved.

Israel's loyalty to the covenant established at Mt. Sinai was constantly tested as she encountered the religions of Canaan. From the time of the conquest into the early monarchy the young nation was much attracted to the religious practices of her pagan neighbors. From Joshua at Shechem to Elijah at Mt. Carmel, instances where the issue of serving the LORD God of Israel was publicly raised, Israel was strangely yet understandably tempted to mix Jahwism with Baalism. This, Elijah lamented, was a forsaking of the commandments of the LORD and a forsaking of his covenant (I Kings 18:18; 19:10, 14). In the struggle for pure Jahwism which continued up to the exile, the trend toward elaboration of worship at temples or shrines dedicated to the LORD appeared, so that the cult of the holy place with an officiating priest became the sign of covenantal loyalty.

This formalistic emphasis on ceremony and cult prevailed during the time of the eighth-century prophets, Amos, Hosea, Isaiah, and Micah. It is noteworthy that these prophets scarcely mention the covenant of Sinai in their drastic criticism of the popular religion of Israel. They did recall God's gracious choice of Israel (Amos 3:2) and God's deliverance of his son out of Egypt (Hos. 11:1), but they did not recall the covenant established with Israel at Mt. Sinai. To understand

this curious omission we have but to see these
prophets in their violent opposition to the routine
performance of external acts of worship which sup-
posedly took the form of keeping the covenant.
Amos therefore inveighed against the pilgrimages
to popular shrines; Hosea denounced the priests
for getting rich off worshippers' sense of guilt;
Isaiah scorned the frequenting of temples and the
offering of prayers; and Micah poured contempt
on offering thousands of rams and ten thousand
rivers of oil. What these prophets wanted instead
of the much displayed rites of worship was a living
relationship to God and a personal concern for the
oppressed and needy. The covenant, as these
prophets observed, had degenerated into a bargain
counter religion in which Israel, through sacrifices
and ritual, purchased from God her license to live
in disregard of human need. Hence it is not difficult to see that these prophets made little use of
the covenant.

In the century following that of the above-
mentioned prophets another attitude which placed
the covenant in high esteem appeared. It was then
that the law book, commonly regarded as
Deuteronomy, which was found in the temple, became the basis for the great reformation under the
direction of King Josiah. The law book was called
the book of the covenant and was read in the hearing of the people (II Kings 23:2). The generation
preceding the reign of Josiah was stigmatized by
the historian as more iniquitous than the Amorites
who formerly inhabited the land (II Kings 21:11).
The law and the covenant which had been Israel's

heritage and tradition had been thoroughly disregarded, so that Judah and Jerusalem had become entirely filled with sin. Thus the demands for a reformation made a return to the law and covenant most necessary. Josiah consequently made the discovered book of the law the basis for the reformation.

Some features of the Sinaitic covenant also appear in Deuteronomy. In both the covenant was identified with the law, and the covenant described the relationship of God to Israel in terms of the redemption from Egypt. However, a significant addition which we do not have in the Exodus account appears in Deuteronomy. This addition is the acknowledgment of the covenant made with Abraham, Isaac, and Jacob. The LORD's choice of Israel to become his people was founded both on his sovereign love for Israel and on his oath sworn to the patriarchs (Deut. 7:8). The possession of the land with its cities and fields was evidence that the LORD remembered the oath to the fathers (6:10-11; 9:5). The covenant with the patriarchs and the covenant at Sinai appeared as interrelated acts of God that set the course of Israel's history within the faithfulness and reliability of God.

At this point in our discussion we ought to review the patriarchal narrative concerning the establishment of the covenant with Abraham. The account (Gen. 17) declares that God, whose name is *El Shaddai,* translated God Almighty, made a covenant with Abram. The covenant's prominent feature involved a promise of a multitude of descendants who would come from Abram and his wife Sarah. Since they were childless and well-advanced in years, the promise of a large posterity was either a mockery or pointed to a miraculous intervention of God in the lives of Abram and Sarah. This intervention did indeed take place and further underscored God's approach to man in establishing the covenant. To confirm the promise of many descendants the name of Abram was changed to Abraham which is made to mean a father of a multitude of nations (17:5). The descendants would comprise kings and nations which would continue into endless generations. The descriptive quality, "everlasting," was attached to the covenant and to the possession of the land in which Abraham moved about as a sojourner. And finally the relationship established between God and Abraham would be continued between God and Abraham's children. In summary, the covenant promised a multitude of descendants, the possession of Canaan, and the continuing bond between God and Abraham's posterity.

The covenant was to be kept, not by obeying the law as in the case of the Sinai covenant, but by the sign of circumcision. This sign, made on all male children at their eighth day and on all foreigners brought within the tribe of Abraham, indicated in their flesh that God's everlasting covenant was upon them.[3]

Deuteronomy associated the oath of God with the covenant he established with Abraham. The oath, as narrated in the Genesis account, involved the repetition of the promise of descendants and the possession of the land (22:16-18; 24:7; 26:3).

65

Although the oath was not given in the setting of the covenant, yet it intended to underscore God's reliability in keeping his covenant. Consequently, as we read of the oath in Deuteronomy (4:31; 7;8,12; 8:1,18) we are in effect reminded of the patriarchal covenant.

Although the Sinaitic covenant is clearly recognized in Deuteronomy (4:13-14), it appears that another covenant with Israel was established in the land of Moab (29:1,9,12,14), forming what would amount to the third in a series of covenants. If this is a correct surmise, then the relationship of God with Israel appears to rest on three pillars which presented Israel's history as having begun with the gracious acts of God to the patriarchs, as having continued with the establishing of Israel as a people, and as stressing the necessity of each new generation's response in faithful and loving obedience to God who keeps covenant and faithfulness toward his people (7:9-11).

The recognition which the prophets Jeremiah and Ezekiel gave to the covenant undoubtedly reflected the influence of Deuteronomy which had inspired the Josiah reformation, although we have no clear indication that either of them took an active part in it. Since the historical narratives do not mention them but only note that Jeremiah composed a lament for the death of Josiah (II Chron. 35:25), we may conclude that they had no active part in the great movement. Jeremiah nevertheless accorded the covenant some significance in his preaching, contrasting the condescending grace of God toward Israel at the time of the Exodus with the base ingratitude revealed in Israel's covenant-breaking. He did not speak of the covenant as the everlasting and continuing relationship between God and Israel. Rather he employed other figures such as the marriage bond, the relationship of father and son, and the shepherd and flock to describe the covenant (Jer. 31:3-4, 9, 20, 32; 23:1-4). Viewed in historical perspective, especially in the post-Josiah period when the gains of the reformation were already lost, the covenant could not be regarded as the enduring bond uniting people with God.

In view of Jeremiah's less than enthusiastic view of the covenantal relationship, we may be somewhat surprised that he nonetheless used the covenant concept to describe the future age of Israel's redemption in the prophecy of the new covenant (31:31-34). The covenant would be established as an act of God's redemptive concern for his people Israel, even as the first covenant expressed God's redemptive love. The law would again be given by God, not written on tables of stone but on the inner self, on the heart. No response needed to be made to the giving of the law as had been the case in the first covenant, for that response would flow spontaneously from the inner self. The knowledge of God, which was indicated in deeds of mercy and justice (cf. 22:15-16), would not be taught because God himself would implant that knowledge in all the people within the covenant. Since sins and iniquities would be fully forgiven, the people would be fully aware of the forgiving grace of God. The emphasis of "I will forgive their iniquities and I will remember their sin no more" would not describe the constant waywardness of the people but rather their constant awareness of God's forgiveness. As a forgiven people living in appreciation of pardon, all would manifest a forgiving compassion for others. In summary, the new covenant presents God in redemptive action patterned on the redemptive act of the Exodus, yet wondrously changed. Here the God-people relationship grows out of God's gracious forgiveness and produces the people's response in demonstrations of forgiveness based on mercy and righteousness, which are the knowledge of God.

The new covenant prophecy of Jeremiah has clear similarities with the Sinai covenant, especially in that both describe the action of God to establish Israel as his people. The terminology of covenant, law, and the God-people bond is common to both. The unique element in the new covenant was not the gracious act of God to redeem his people, but rather the taking into account of Israel's inability to obey the law and to keep the covenant. As Jeremiah pondered the history of Israel's faithlessness to the LORD who had redeemed her, as he saw that covenantal renewal or reformation was like the morning dew which quickly vanishes away, he declared that mankind as seen in Israel was so corrupt and perverse that it would be impossible for Israel to be obedient and faithful to any covenant which God might make with her. The prophet as appointed tester of the ways of Israel (6:27) declared that "the heart is deceitful above all things, and desperately corrupt;

who can understand it?" (17:9). So it becomes impossible for Israel to change her ways and to return to fellowship with God, even as it would be impossible for an Ethiopian to change his skin and a leopard his spots (13:23). Any covenant requiring the obedience of the people has no chance for survival; it carries its own seeds of failure. Jeremiah, more than any prophet before him, had clearly discerned the problem of man's inability to remain within the covenantal fellowship of God.[4]

Ezekiel shared Jeremiah's "low" view of the sinfulness of Israel and her consequent inability to keep the law as seen in a review of Israel's history (ch. 20). Israel was called a "house of rebellion" (2:7). Because of Israel's sinful disposition this prophet projected the future restoration of Israel in terms of inner cleansing and change. "A new heart I will give you, and a new spirit I will put within you; and I will take out of your flesh the heart of stone and give you a heart of flesh" (36:26). The inner disposition would be changed radically by the implanting of a new spirit. The new spirit would create the ability to walk according to the ordinances of God. Ezekiel, like Jeremiah, saw no restoration of covenantal fellowship based on the requirements of Deuteronomy or of the Sinaitic covenant. The new fellowship would have its base in the creation of a new heart and in the giving of a new spirit.[5]

In the reference quoted above, Ezekiel did not use the term covenant for the new relationship between God and Israel. It was for the vindication of his holy name rather than out of regard for his

69

covenant that the LORD would bring back all the dispersed out of the lands in which the name of God had been profaned. The honor of the LORD had been reviled by nations who declared, "These are the people of the LORD, and yet they had to go out of his land" (36:20), and the restoration would be a response to this.

However, in other instances (34:25; 37:26), Ezekiel prophesied the establishing of "the covenant of peace," which implied the perfect welfare of Israel in a future time characterized by abundant fertility of fields, freedom from slavery, and blessed welfare in all relationships. Ezekiel thus filled out the new covenant utterance of Jeremiah with some practical details concerning common life. We may here underscore a previous observation that the forgiveness of God would be constantly kept in mind in the people's response to God and in their behavior to others. The prophet did not envision a "sinless" people who would enjoy the covenant of peace, but rather a people whose sin would always be forgiven. This people would be filled with the spirit of forgiveness and would demonstrate forgiveness and compassion to others in that new covenant community.

In our survey of the place of the covenant in the future hopes of Israel we need to discuss the covenant made with David. The occasion which led to the establishing of this covenant was David's desire to build a house for the ark of God, which was then kept in a tent. The narration of the event (II Sam. 7) states that David had overcome his enemies and was living in his house of cedar. The king's desire to build a house for the ark of the LORD was communicated to Nathan the prophet, who at first encouraged him to do as he desired. During that night the word of the LORD instructed Nathan to tell David that he should not build the house he had planned but that his son would do that. The main point of Nathan's message was that the LORD and not David would build a house which would be the house or lineage of David to be established on the throne of Israel. In this interesting play on the word "house" we discern that the LORD was establishing a special relationship with David, a relationship which had all the basic elements of a covenant: God's choice of David, his favor which prospered David, his promise of faithfulness to David's descendants, and the establishing of his throne forever. Even though all these covenantal features are present in the narrative, the word "covenant" does not appear. Why the historian should refrain from using it here is not easy to determine. Apparently the Deuteronomist narrator intended to restrict the use of the word to the relationship of God either to the patriarchs (II Kings 13:23), or to Israel at the time of the Exodus (I Kings 8:21; II Kings 17:15; 23:2-3). It was for later writers such as the Chronicler and psalmists to declare that God had indeed established an eternal covenant with David (II Chron. 7:18; 13:5; 21:7; Ps. 89:28,34,39 [29,35,40]; 132:11-12). The psalm (II Sam. 23:1-7) is known as the last words of David, in which the words, "For he has made with me an everlasting covenant," reflect the time of the

Chronicler when the relationship God established with David was readily described as a covenant.

The above psalm, with its reference to the everlasting covenant, may have been the inspiration for Psalm 89 which enthusiastically celebrates the covenant with David. Covenantal vocabulary, which is so strangely absent and restricted in II Samuel 7, now comes to full expression in such words as *ḥesedh*, "steadfast love," *'emûnah*, "faithfulness," *'ôlam*, "everlasting," and *shaba'*, "swear." A significant and unique feature in this covenant description is that its endurability is compared with the sun, moon, and skies (89:36-37), a comparison which also appears in Jeremiah under the terms of a covenant with the day and the night (33:19-21).

Extolling the covenant is not the primary purpose in this psalm, for the praise of the covenant becomes the background upon which the psalmist projects his moving lament. He greatly deplores that God has renounced his covenant, for God has manifested his wrath to bring dishonor upon the king, the descendant of David. King and city have been despoiled by the enemy, and the glory of David's throne has been cast to the ground. All this appears to reflect the time of Judah's exile when Jerusalem was destroyed and the king was taken captive. However, out of the lament the psalmist calls on God to remember his steadfast love, his faithfulness, and his oath which are the tokens of the covenant made with David. Hope arises out of the lament, for God will surely not forget the covenant once established with David.

Israel's future hope lies in the restoration of that covenant (**cf.** also Ps. 132).

Deutero-Isaiah, the prophet of the exile, appeared on the stage of Israel's history when her glory and fame had vanished. The nation languished overcome with despair in the Babylonian captivity. Some of her godly-minded people were deeply conscious of her sin and guilt and accepted the disgrace of the exile as God's just visitation upon them. The more secular among them followed the instructions of Jeremiah (29:1-7) and established themselves in the life and commerce of Babylon so that they had little concern for the restoration of the chosen people. In Babylon's mighty grip Israel's national hopes had reached their nadir; in that dark night she saw no dawn of hope. Yet in that darkness the great prophet of the exile arose to proclaim that God's dawn would break in upon the night and herald the beginning of a new day.

This prophet had pondered with careful discernment the records of God's redemptive acts in Israel's history. The traditions, both written and oral, declared that God had entered history to act on behalf of Israel to establish her as a people and a kingdom so that she might mediate the blessings of God to the nations of the world. It is both remarkable and significant that the prophet alludes to three special occasions when God established relationships in which the covenant played a prominent part. These are the covenants with Abraham, with Israel through Moses, and with David.

The prophet refers to Abraham twice. The

73

first reference, "But you, Israel, my servant, Jacob, whom I have chosen, the offspring of Abraham, my friend" (41:8), intends to parallel God's call of Israel to be his servant with the call of her forebear Abraham. The second, "look to the rock from which you were hewn, and to the quarry from which you were digged. Look to Abraham your father and to Sarah who bore you; for when he was but one I called him, and I blessed him and made him many" (51:1b-2), stresses the calling of Abraham from an unpromising origin, yet in spite of this God blessed him to make him many. Although the prophet does not mention the covenant made with Abraham, yet he and his hearers, then living at the place of Abraham's origin, would be reminded of the oath and promise which God made to Abraham when he established the covenant.

Although neither Moses nor the Exodus is named, the prophet makes clear allusions to the Exodus history. The highway prepared through the desert (40:3) recalls the way Israel took when she left Egypt; the thirsty drinking water from the rock (48:21) alludes to the people quenching their thirst during their wilderness journey; and the destroying of Rahab at the sea and the drying up of the great deep (51:9-10) pictures the great deliverance of Israel's crossing the Red Sea. Further, in the descriptions of the Servant of the Lord the prophet alludes to Moses as a teacher (50:4; 53:11), as a man of the spirit (42:1), and as an intercessor (53:12).

The prophet of the exile makes but one reference to David and the covenant. "Incline your ear, and come to me; hear, that your soul may live; and I will make with you an everlasting covenant, my steadfast, sure love for David" (55:3). Here we find the full covenant vocabulary used: *'ôlam,* "eternal," *ḥesedh,* "steadfast love," and *'emûnah,* "faithful," here given in the niphal participial form. David's covenant as described in Psalm 89 is here compressed into one line. The prophet thus points out that even though David's line was not on the throne yet God had not forgotten the covenant. The covenant shall again be restored, not with a representative of David's house, but with David's people then in exile, for they are being addressed in this context. The Lord shall bring the trustworthy benefits of the Davidic covenant upon the weary exiles who shall become a witness and an attraction to the nations (55:4-5). The covenantal blessings are here interpreted messianically and are to be realized in the future ministry of the redeemed people.

The exiles, who are referred to as a widow forsaken by her husband, are comforted to know that although the LORD in overflowing wrath had for a brief moment forsaken them, he will now gather them with great compassion to restore them to their land. Much like the restoration of the earth after the flood in the days of Noah, so shall Israel experience the faithfulness of the LORD, for his "covenant of peace" shall not be removed from her (54:10). The association of peace, *shalom,* with the covenant points out the welfare and good which the covenant relationship is designed to promote.

This covenant carries with it the bestowal of the LORD's spirit, which was placed upon the Servant (42:1), and which now through the mediation or mission of the Servant is also upon the redeemed community (59:21). Moreover, the words of the LORD, formerly placed in the mouth of the prophets (Jer. 1:9) and in the mouth of the Servant (Isa. 49:2; 50:4), are now put in the mouth of the restored people. Furthermore, the covenant people are assured that the spirit and the word of God, formerly the tokens of prophetic revelation, would continue to be present in their descendants. Besides, the eunuch who is faithful within the community shall enjoy a recognition beyond that of one with many sons and daughters; and the foreigner shall likewise participate in the covenantal blessings (56:4-7). The covenant shall extend to many generations and those formerly excluded shall fully share in all the covenantal benefits of the redeemed community.

In two other instances Deutero-Isaiah makes use of the covenant to be realized in a similar futuristic manner. "I have given you as a covenant to the people, a light to the nations, to open the eyes that are blind, to bring out the prisoners from the dungeon, from the prison those who sit in darkness" (42:6b-7). From the context we learn that the Servant of the LORD is here addressed. The Servant's identity, which in the history of interpretation of Deutero-Isaiah has received much discussion, may be both Israel the people of God and an individual of messianic import. The Servant has been made a covenant which is in effect a

God-ordained mission to bring light to the nations, sight to the blind, and freedom to prisoners. The other reference declares that, "I have kept you and given you as a covenant to the people, to establish the land, to apportion the desolate heritages; saying to the prisoners, 'Come forth,' to those who are in darkness, 'Appear' " (49:8-9). This last passage rather clearly describes the return of the captives to their homeland. However, the full context looks for people coming from many distant places to enjoy the favor and blessings of the LORD. In both instances the covenant carries within itself a task more than a relationship. This task placed upon the Servant includes on the one hand the return of Israel from her exile and on the other hand the bringing of God's light and revelation to nations beyond the community of Israel.

In the above survey of the use which the prophet made or did not make of the covenants established in Israel's history we ought to determine from the little data what significance the covenant had in his preaching. In his references to Abraham he made no mention of the covenant or promise as a possible God-given assurance for Israel's return to her homeland as did the psalmist (Ps. 105:8-10, 42; 106:45-47). Likewise, in his more frequent allusions to the history of the Exodus, the covenant established at Sinai was not mentioned. Although mentioned but once, the Davidic covenant with its everlasting faithfulness of God shall again come into being. In this covenant the Servant people shall become a witness and shall attract many nations because of the LORD their God. This

77

covenant, formerly established with David and his house, is now to be established with David's people, here called Servant. In this covenant we can clearly detect that a double purpose was to be realized: The first was that the special favor of God, once promised to David and his house, shall now come upon the Servant people; and the second was that the Servant people were to be appointed for mission to the nations. The second purpose was plainly stated in 42:6 and 49:8 where the Servant has become the covenant, that is, the ministry of God to the peoples. This double usage of covenant may be stated as follows: *God makes his covenant with the Servant, and God makes the Servant himself his covenant.*

Deutero-Isaiah therefore made a significant transition in the understanding of covenant, which has become identified with the mission of the Servant. We can best understand covenant as we come to know the ministry of the Servant.

As described by the prophet this ministry reached universal proportions that surpassed the concepts of former prophets. Previously, Isaiah (2:2-4) and Micah (4:1-2) had envisaged the nations going to Mount Zion to hear the word of the LORD and to be taught his ways. The Servant, however, has been appointed to bring justice, *mishpat,* which may mean practical religion, to the nations (42:1). These nations are waiting to receive his law, *torah,* possibly meaning instruction (42:4). The Servant's ministry is not to be restricted to Israel for her restoration and salvation, for that would be too small a task; his ministry shall

78

bring light and salvation to the ends of the earth (49:6). Also in the Davidic covenant passage it is stated that this Servant shall become a witness that shall attract many nations (55:4-5). Further, many nations and kings, as they gaze upon the spectacle of the Suffering Servant in dumb amazement (52:15), shall be told that the suffering of the Righteous One shall be for the forgiveness and healing of sinful people, and that by his knowledge the many shall be declared righteous (53:11). The Servant's ministry will bring the revelation of God to the nations, and through his vicarious suffering the nations will experience the forgiving and healing grace of God.

This vicarious suffering will be the apex of the Servant's covenantal ministry. Here we observe that the covenant becomes more than God's gracious favor established with Israel in the giving of the law at Mount Sinai, for the covenant expresses itself in terms of an individual who identifies himself with Israel and the nations in terms of suffering and affliction. The covenant thus becomes a bond in life which takes hold of mankind in the depth of human need. That need, as seen in the breaking and forsaking of covenants in Israel's past, was the restoration and healing of a rebellious people. To be sure, God in his faithfulness and his steadfast love did remember his covenant and did restore his people. But now this restoration will mean more than a return to the beloved Jerusalem; it will mean that Israel shall be restored into a covenantal fellowship which rests upon forgiveness mediated through the vicarious atonement of the Servant. Covenant therefore has become more than a formal contract or ratified agreement between God and Israel; it has become a person whose life of teaching and vicarious suffering brings God's peace and healing upon a sinful and broken people.

A brief resumé of our study may help summarize the significance of the covenant and its development in the Old Testament.

1. The covenant was instituted by God in history. The relationship between the LORD and Israel was never regarded as a natural bond that united a nation with her god. Ancient religions frequently speak of tribes which had been united to their gods by a natural bond arising from a myth in which the tribe or clan was considered to be offspring from its god. Although in a few instances the LORD is called the father of Israel and Israel is called son, in no instance could Israel claim to be related to her God by ties of birth. In every case of the covenant, such as with Abraham, or with Israel, or with David, God established a bond with people who were in no way "naturally" related to him. God chose people who had no more claim to this privilege than any other and brought them into the covenant.

The covenant took place in Israel's history and at significant points in that history. The covenant with Abraham was instituted after the breakdown of human history at Babel, and this marked the beginning of redemptive history. The covenant with Israel took place at the deliverance from Egypt, at the beginning of Israel's history as a people. The covenant with David happened when Israel was established as a kingdom and when the center of worship and of the state was placed in Jerusalem. The new covenant, or the covenant for the end time with its roots in covenantal history, anticipates the consummation of history when a renewed and Spirit-filled people shall fully realize the benefits of the covenant. Thus it is that the covenant in the Old Testament underscores the redemption and revelation of God in the events of Israel's history.

2. The covenant demonstrates the LORD's election of Israel for mission. This may be seen in the covenant established with Abraham which embodied God's promise that all the families of the earth should be blessed. This promise implied that the covenanted seed of Abraham would be the channel of blessing and would become God's mission for redemptive history in the world (Gen. 12:2-3; 17:4-6; 18:18; 22:18). At Sinai Israel was designated to be a "kingdom of priests" (Ex. 19:6), which in effect placed Israel in the world to represent the God of the covenant to the nations. Israel's law, known as the book of the covenant, was to be her wisdom among the nations (Deut. 4:6), who would flow to Jerusalem in the final days to be instructed in the law (Is. 2:2-4). Covenant was equated with mission in the descriptions of the Servant of the LORD who would bring restoration to Israel and the light of salvation to the ends of the earth (Is. 49:6).

3. In its legal obligations the covenant could be distorted into formalism. When Israel was en-

joined to keep the covenant by obeying the law formalism became a tempting possibility. Preoccupation with the requirements of the law did indeed lead to cultic formalism that reduced the covenant to a "bargain-counter" religion in which God's favor was thought to be regulated according to the magnificence of ceremonial observances. During the time of the eighth-century prophets the covenant had been degraded to a *"Do ut des"* (I give that you may give) performance which produced an irreverent calculation of winning God's favor rather than a trustful surrender to his covenantal faithfulness.

4. Israel's breaking of the covenant did not destroy the relationship which God had established. The keeping or the breaking of the covenant posed a serious problem in the relationship between God and Israel. The keeping of the covenant could, and in some instances did, produce a legalism which destroyed the inner graces of compassion and righteousness, as we have noted in the preceding paragraph. However, the wanton breaking of the covenant in worshipping other gods raised the problem of the covenant's durability. And this problem arose shortly after the Sinai covenant had been consummated when Israel worshipped the golden calf. God's wrath was aroused and he threatened to destroy Israel. However, the destruction was changed to a plague, which was sent upon the people (Ex. 32:35). This Sinai incident became a pattern, a cycle of wrath, punishment, and restoration, which historians used as they narrated Israel's covenant-breaking in the case of the Achan incident

(Josh. 7:11,15), in the defeat during the time of the Judges (Josh. 23:16; Judg. 2:20), in the case of Solomon's apostasy (I Kings 11:11), and in the going into exile (II Kings 17:15-18).

Israel's breaking of the covenant brought on punishment, but in no instance was the covenant abrogated by the LORD. "Man cannot annul the covenant; if he breaks it, this only means that he is violating its conditions. The majesty of divine love shows itself in this, that God alone has the power to dissolve the relationship, yet never makes use of it."[6]

Israel's conduct, whether it be covenant-breaking or covenant-forsaking, would not cause the LORD to abandon his people (Deut. 4:31). As transgressor Israel came under the chastisement of God, as was the case with the exile. Yet chastisement was not the end of the covenantal relationship, for Israel's restoration came about through the LORD's remembering the covenant. Covenant-breaking, therefore, was never ignored, since to do so would call the LORD's ethical integrity into question. Moreover, covenant-keeping, to which Israel was constantly enjoined, could not become the base on which the covenant relationship rested, for this would promote self-righteousness, an attitude of heart not acceptable in the God-Israel relationship (cf. Deut. 8:17-18; 9:4-6). We may consequently observe that, on the one hand, the giving of the covenant gave proper recognition to both God's moral integrity and to his bestowal of grace upon a sinful people, and that, on the other hand, Israel in her relationship with God was always commanded both to keep the covenant through moral living, and to receive the covenant and all its benefits as bestowals of God's favor, thereby keeping herself free from self-righteousness.

5. The new covenant for the end time would bring about inner renewal. The descriptions given by Jeremiah emphasized the writing of the law on the heart, the inner self, which is to say that God would implant his ideals and ways for life within man. Ezekiel spoke of a new spirit, and a heart of flesh instead of a heart of stone; by this he meant a ready receptivity for the revelation and instruction of God. God would freely grant forgiveness, which implies that perfection of life would not be achieved. Yet forgiveness would qualify all "to know" God. This knowledge, which could not be imparted by the formal teaching of priests, would be expressed in deeds of compassion and justice. The community envisaged by these prophets would apparently not be free from human frailty and error, yet the appreciation of forgiveness and the inner direction of the will would bring about the conditions of peace.

6. The Servant of the Lord in Deutero-Isaiah would be God's covenant for Israel and the nations. It is significant to note that here the covenant is not an agreement, but a person, the Servant. We are told that this Servant receives the covenantal benefits once promised to David, and that the Servant himself becomes the covenant in his ministry to Israel and the nations. This mission includes the giving of the torah, as was also true in

Jeremiah's new covenant; but his mission goes further in that he shall bring salvation and deliverance to those in prisons of darkness. His ministry shall astonish kings and nations, who shall gaze in dumb amazement at the despised and afflicted Servant. They shall learn that the Servant thus despised and afflicted suffers for those who despise him. It is through his chastisement that peace and healing shall come upon Israel and the many. In the hymn of joy which follows chapter fifty-three, the prophet declares that "the LORD's covenant of peace" (54:10) shall not be removed from the people. Peace, which connoted the fullness of God's favor in all areas of life, shall be the eternal possession of the redeemed people. Truly the Servant as covenant shall accomplish fully what other covenants realized only in part. This is God's covenant at its highest fruition.

The Covenant at Qumran

The concept of covenant played an important role in the monastic community at Qumran established in the Judean wilderness west of the Dead Sea at the close of the second century B.C. This community was founded by priests banished from Jerusalem by the Hasmonean priesthood, descendants of the Maccabean priest-kings, who were in political power. The exiled priests set up a monastic order under rigorous regulations derived from the law of Moses. As interpreted by the Qumran priests the law became the framework of the covenant which everyone entering the community placed himself under oath to obey.

The references to the covenant in the writings of Qumran regard the covenant either as the continuation of the Old Testament covenant or as the new covenant. The covenant made with the patriarchs is thought to be indissoluble; however, it is to be remembered that Israel constantly forsook the covenant so that only the remnant, the elect of God, remained within it. The restoration of some Jews to Jerusalem after the Babylonian exile becomes the basis of the Qumran teaching concerning covenant and remnant. As God saw the penitence and purity of heart of the remnant, and remembered his covenant to bring back his people, so he remembers the penitent and faithful remnant of his people to establish them in his covenant. The counterpart to this understanding of the covenant is that the rest of the Jews have no part in the fellowship of the sons of light, but are the sons of darkness who are destined to come under the judgment of God. The monastics at Qumran thus regarded themselves as the preserved remnant with whom God was continuing his covenant.

Poverty was a sign of faithfulness to the covenant. According to the teachings of the sect unchastity and desire for material riches were the sins that brought on the downfall of the apostates who were once within the covenant. The newly admitted members were obliged to surrender their personal property into the control of the community. The readiness with which the new member would surrender his goods was an indication of being in a state of grace and he could therefore be identified with the group. Thus it appears that the poor in worldly goods were very similar to the "poor in spirit," which is to say that poverty brought on humility and that riches encouraged pride. The future glory of the community would be brought on through the poor, for God would demonstrate his power through their weakness as they waged the war of vengeance against the enemies of God. In the not-too-distant future God would use these members of his covenant to exterminate all the heathen nations and to bring punishment upon the apostates who no longer lived within the covenant.

The title "new covenant" appears at least twice in their literature, which would indicate that the prophetic ideal of Jeremiah (31:31-34) was in their thinking. Further, they speak of "the covenant of steadfast love" (ḥesed) and "the covenant of repentance," which seem to refer to the prophecies of Jeremiah and Ezekiel. If they indeed considered this to be the new covenant, it was not instituted at the organization of their community, for they refer to the followers of the man of the lie who had previously rejected the covenant of God in the land of Damascus. It seems clear, therefore, that the new covenant had already come into existence before they withdrew to the wilderness, and that they were the faithful remnant of that new covenant.[7]

The use of covenant at Qumran to describe the God-people relationship has a remarkable affinity to the concept of covenant in the New Testament. As we shall see in the next part of this chapter, the relationship of God with the church came through Jesus Christ who was the mediator of the new covenant. As at Qumran, the people of God in the New Testament were the members of that new covenant. However, the difference between Qumran and the New Testament on the point of covenant is extremely interesting and important. For the monastics in the Judean wilderness, the new covenant was in existence before they were driven from Jerusalem and were established in communal life. They carried on the true line of the new covenant; the rest of the Jews were apostates. In contrast, the New Testament declares that the new covenant came into being through Jesus Christ. Further, Qumran as the community of the new covenant was awaiting the coming of the messiah, or more accurately the messiahs; the New Testament confessed that Jesus of Nazareth was the messiah who had come to institute the new covenant. Perhaps the most noteworthy difference appears in the particularism of the Qumran covenant which restricted membership in the covenant to the ascetics at the monastery, as compared to the universalism of the New Testament covenant which embraced all Jews and Gentiles who, through faith in Jesus Christ, became heirs of the covenant and promise made to Abraham (Gal. 3:16-29). Thus, at Qumran the members of the sect entered the covenant of God and awaited the coming of the promised messiah; in the New Testament all believers as members of the church were in the new covenant because the messiah had come and had established it.

It becomes clear, therefore, that the New Testament emphasis on the covenant not merely highlights the expected realization of a new God-people relationship, but also contradicts the claims of Qumran to be the people of the covenant. The authentic continuation of the Old Testament covenant is not to be found in the monastic community but in the church established by Jesus Christ through the apostles.

The Covenant in the New Testament

The New Testament, which may more accurately be called New Covenant (cf. title page of English versions of the New Testament), makes use of the word "covenant" only thirty-three times, of which seventeen appear in the Epistle to the Hebrews. Apart from Hebrews the covenant is given incidental attention, which is especially to be noticed in contrast to words like "law," "righteousness," and "holiness." However, the idea of covenant as descriptive of a God-people relationship was not ignored, for this relationship appears frequently and under different names and descriptions.

In the Epistle to the Hebrews the author's thesis is that the new covenant of which Christ is the Mediator is better than the old covenant mediated through Moses. The new covenant passage of Jeremiah is quoted in full and in the author's line of argument yields the conclusion that the old covenant is obsolete and ready to vanish away (8:8-13). The new covenant is superior to the old since it is enacted on better promises (8:6), and since the blood of the sacrifice of Christ secures eternal redemption which is also effective for those under the first covenant (9:12,15). The sacrifice of Christ is made but once under the new covenant, for the words of the Old Testament prophecy state that God will no longer remember the sins and misdeeds of his people (10:11-18). In these covenant passages we learn that the author intends to contrast the new covenant established in Christ with the old covenant given through Moses, according to the interpretation derived from the new covenant prophecy of Jeremiah.

In the writings of the apostle Paul the covenant does not receive such formal treatment as he gives to themes such as righteousness. In his references to the covenant Paul relates it to the promises made in the Old Testament which have come to fruition in the Gospel. This means that Jew and Gentile alike have the eschatological hope for both the future and the present in this world. Since Paul does not delineate the covenant, we may assume that he has all the covenants in mind (Eph. 2:12). These covenants and promises are a much-to-be-appreciated heritage (Rom. 9:4). Similarly, in Galatians Paul relates promise to covenant, in this case to the covenant with Abraham. The point to be made is that, in giving the law 430 years later, God did not annul the promise made to Abraham (3:16-18). Paul does not mention the covenant with its attendant promise at the giving of the law since he is establishing the theme of Abraham's righteousness by faith. The other use

90

of covenant in Galatians has a figurative sense by which Paul differentiates between the freedom of those in the church and the servitude of those in Judaism (4:24-26). In his discussion about a letter of recommendation, a letter which he declares to be written for him on the hearts of the members of the church at Corinth, Paul is quite naturally led to think about being ministers of the new covenant since the new covenant speaks of the law being written on the heart. This new covenant with its special kind of writing induces Paul to contrast the life-giving writing of the Spirit on the heart with the external writing of the law on tablets of stone, which writing brings death (II Cor. 3:1-7). The ministers of the new covenant, therefore, possess the Spirit whose writing on the heart results in life. In the Apostle's extended consideration of Israel's place in the purpose of God (Rom. 9-11), he combines a covenant-deliverance passage (Is. 59:20-21) with the passage from Jeremiah concerning the forgiveness of sins found in the new covenant, in order to establish the point that all Israel shall be saved (Rom. 11:26-27).

Finally we need to examine the use made of covenant in Jesus' institution of the Last Supper. In Mark Jesus declares "This is my blood of the covenant poured out for many" (14:24). To this Matthew adds, "for the forgiveness of sins" (26:28). In both gospels the adjective "new" which appears in late manuscripts is not found in the early manuscripts. The intrusion of this "new" covenant in the later manuscripts may be due to Paul's version of the institution: "This cup is the new covenant in my blood" (I Cor. 11:25), a text which has no variant reading. If we may regard the Mark-Matthew text with its omission of the adjective "new" as the earliest tradition, then we may not have an allusion to the new covenant prophecy of Jeremiah. And it may well be that in the use of the word "covenant" Jesus did not intend to allude to Jeremiah, for other prominent features of Jeremiah's oracle such as the writing of the law on the heart, the knowledge of God, and the God-people relationship are conspicuously absent in the institution of the Last Supper. Moreover, the breaking of the bread and the pouring of the cup with their symbolic interpretations as the broken body and the poured out blood are not found in Jeremiah. To be sure, the "for the forgiveness of sins" found in the Matthean version may reflect Jeremiah's "I will forgive their iniquity, and I will remember their sin no more" (31:34). However, the theme of forgiveness of sins can equally well be related to other Old Testament references as will be done below. Our preliminary observation about the covenant in the Last Supper is that it may not refer to the new covenant oracle of Jeremiah. The covenant that comes into clear focus is that prophesied by Deutero-Isaiah about the Servant whom God had set as a covenant for Israel and the nations. Jesus had previously identified himself with the servant of the LORD in that he had forewarned his disciples of his rejection, death, and resurrection (Mark 8:31). The anointing of Jesus at Bethany for burial, as he interpreted it, and the plotting for the betrayal continued the theme of the Servant rejected and put to death. At the supper itself Jesus employs the bread and the cup as symbols for his suffering and death which reflect the suffering and death of the Servant. The body broken like bread and the blood poured out like the cup depict one much like the great Sufferer in Isaiah 53. Since the Servant motif dominates the setting and the institution of the Last Supper, the covenant mentioned in it would be that spoken of by Deutero-Isaiah. As we noted above, the prophet of the exile had declared that the LORD had set the Servant as a covenant, which was to say that the covenant was the mission of the Servant. If we understand covenant as mission, then Jesus is here stating, through the symbolism of the cup, the pouring out of his blood, that he is accomplishing the mission of the Suffering Servant. Matthew's addition, "for the forgiveness of sins," emphasizes the portrait of the Servant who makes himself an offering for sin and bears the sins of many.

As given by Jesus in the institution of the Holy Supper the covenant reflects and fulfills the covenantal mission of the Servant. The Sinaitic covenant on which the Jewish passover was established has here given way to a covenant concept which is more than the bond between God and people, for, as the prophet of the exile has made clear, this covenant is the mission in which the Servant offers himself as the ransom for many. This mission has universal dimensions which the covenant in the Last Supper brings to consummation through the pouring out of the Servant's blood.

In summary, the Old Testament covenants come into fulfillment and fruition as they are incorporated in particular themes of New Testament writers. Since promise and covenant are parts of the same fabric in the Old Testament, the blessings of Abraham's covenant are promises of God realized through faith in Christ. The believers are children of Abraham who inherit the promises made to the patriarch. The Sinaitic covenant represents a Judaism which must give way to the new covenant as foretold by Jeremiah. This fits in with the thesis of Hebrews which shows that the dispensation of Jesus Christ far exceeds the servants and service of the dispensation of the old covenant. Although the Davidic covenant is not mentioned in the New Testament, it may well be included in the Servant covenant of Deutero-Isaiah (Is. 55:3). The high point of covenant consummation involves the Servant whose covenantal ministry Jesus took upon himself and meaningfully symbolized in the institution of the Last Supper.

NOTES

1. G. E. Mendenhall, *Law and Covenant in Israel and the Ancient Near East* (Pittsburgh: The Biblical Colloquium, 1955); "Covenant," *The Interpreter's Dictionary of the Bible*, A-D (Nashville: Abingdon Press, 1962), pp. 714-15.

2. The LORD is a translation of THE Name of God associated with the giving of the covenant at Mt. Sinai. The Hebrew consonants without vowels are YHWH. With vowels the spelling becomes Yahweh or Jahweh.

Translators have generally preferred the translation, the LORD, to the transliteration of the Hebrew, Yahweh. The LXX has *KURIOS* and the Vulgate *DOMINUS*, both meaning the LORD. The English versions have the same translation—except the American Revised Version (1901), which has Jehovah.

Yahweh is built on the verbal root *HYH*, the verb "to be," which suggests the background meaning of the Existing One, or the One Causing to Be, derived from the causative stem of the verb. The extensive literature about the Name and its meaning produces no consensus, although most scholars accept one of the above derivations. The interpretation taken from the causative stem, the One Causing to Be, or the One Bringing into Existence, has much to commend it since at Mt. Sinai the LORD brought into existence the nation of Israel and established his covenant with her.

3. The Sinaitic covenant also had a sign which was the sabbath (Ex. 31:13-17).

4. Cf. G. von Rad, *Old Testament Theology*, Vol. II (London: Oliver and Boyd, 1965), pp. 216-17.

5. *Ibid.*, pp. 270-71.

6. W. Eichrodt, *Theology of the Old Testament*, Vol. I (Philadelphia: The Westminster Press, 1961), p. 54.

7. The teachings on the covenant and the remnant are prominent in the following writings of the sect: *The Damascus Document* and *The Manual of Discipline*. Translations are given by M. Burrows, *The Dead Sea Scrolls* (New York: The Viking Press, 1955). For a discussion on the covenant theology at Qumran read K. Schubert, *The Dead Sea Community* (New York: Harper & Brothers, 1959), pp. 80-88; also A.R.C. Leaney, *The Rule of Qumran and Its Meaning* (Philadelphia: The Westminster Press, 1966), pp. 119 ff.

CHAPTER IV

RIGHTEOUSNESS AND SALVATION

"A TWENTIETH-CENTURY READER ENCOUNTERING the word righteousness in Semitic texts must always be careful to adjust his thought and not to place this term in the categories to which our word righteousness has accustomed us."[1] These cautionary words may well apply to any study of Old Testament terms but they are especially appropriate for the study of righteousness. We are accustomed to associate righteousness with some kind of impartial and impersonal dispensing of reward and blame by which the moral rectitude of society is maintained. In the Old Testament righteousness does have something of our modern concept of justice, but it cannot be restricted to that, for we will find to our surprise that other concepts have important significance for understanding it. As we shall see, the word "righteousness" shines forth in a spectrum of meaning that cannot be reduced to one line of thought. It behooves the student of the Old Testament, as well as of the New Testament, to free himself from any kind of bondage, whether it be an adherence to prevailing scholastic categories of thought or a reaction against them.

The meaning of the verbal root *SDQ* from which the noun "righteousness" is derived can best be defined as conformity to a norm.[2] This norm, however, is not to be construed as some universal ideal which serves as a yardstick to determine the righteousness of a person or thing. The norm for righteousness arises out of a relationship, either between God and man, or between man and man. The Old Testament often sets these relationships within the framework of a covenant. Conduct can then be considered righteous as it conforms to the requirements of the covenant. Righteousness consequently is not primarily a conformity to ethical standards or moral laws. Insofar as ethics or laws are part of a covenantal relationship they may help determine the norm for covenantal conduct. Covenantal standards, however, involve more than ethics since they require the loyalty and faithfulness of those within the covenant. The norm is thus determined by what the relationship demands. In Ecclesiastes (7:15-16) the Preacher warns against being overmuch righteous because conforming rigidly to one standard overlooks the fact that the same standard may not obtain in every case. Consequently, conformity to a norm, as Kautzsch pointed out, does not imply uniformity of norm.

Weights and measurements, for example, are instruments of righteousness when they conform to the standards used in business relationships (Lev. 19:36; Ezek. 45:10). The sacrifices of righteousness are those offered in accordance with the requirements of the covenant (Ps. 4:6 [5]; 51:21 [19]). Righteousness is usually associated with conduct,

97

which means that conduct is regarded righteous to the degree that it conforms to the relationship in question. Samaria and Sodom, known for their wickedness, are declared to be more righteous than Jerusalem because the grievous sin of Jerusalem has made her sinful sisters appear righteous (Ezek. 16:51-52). Judah declares that Tamar who disguised herself as a harlot to seduce him was more righteous than he because she had waited in vain for her deceased husband's brother in order to preserve the name of her deceased husband (Gen. 38:26; **cf.** Deut. 25:5-10). She had been obedient to the requirements of the levirate law that required the deceased husband's brother to marry his widow in order to prevent the blotting out of the name of her first husband. Because she kept that law and because Judah had neglected to do what the law required, Tamar was more righteous than Judah.

In some cases righteousness in conduct went beyond what the relationship required. In the instance of Saul, who declared that David was more righteous than he had been, he meant that David had not only honored the relationship of king-subject but had also spared the life of Saul, who had broken the king-subject relationship by regarding David as a subversive and a fugitive (I Sam. 24:17). David was more righteous than his sovereign because of his faithfulness even though the king had violated all claims to David's loyalty (26:21-23). The righteous man will go beyond legal correctness in his relationships to show

kindness and compassion where they are needed
(Prov. 12:10; 21:26; 29:7).

Attitude of mind as well as performance of
deeds took on special significance in the description of the righteous man. In Psalm 1 the righteous delights in the law of God, and finds joy in
meditating on it (**cf.** Ps. 119:47-48). Psalms 15
and 24, known as the liturgies of the gate since
they are addressed to the worshippers entering the
gate of the temple, declare that those with clean
hands, a pure heart, and a desire to seek God shall
receive blessings and righteousness (24:5), that is to
say, they shall receive acceptance within the
covenant community (**cf.** Jesus' use of "righteous"
in the parable of the Pharisee and the publican,
Lk. 18:9-14). Righteousness therefore involves the
intent of the heart as well as the deed of the hand.

In the sermon of Ezekiel (18:5-24) righteousness is related to the keeping of the commandments of God, which is described as a day-by-day
personal responsibility. Righteousness is not a
family heritage which can be passed on from father to son, nor is it a position or goal that once
achieved remains inviolate. The man who faithfully keeps the commands of the LORD each day
is righteous and shall surely live within the
covenant relationship (**cf.** Deut. 6:25; 24:13).
The question of keeping the law perfectly, or the
necessity of forgiveness of sin was not raised, **for**
righteousness was more an avowal to keep the law
than a declaration to keep it perfectly. The psalmist's loud cries for vindication according to his
righteousness (7:9 [8]; 17:1-5; 18:21-25 [20-24];

99

26:1-3), which irritate the ears of Christian people who under Pauline instruction can claim no righteousness of their own, must be understood as an appeal to the integrity of his heart to do the commands of God. The Old Testament man made no distinction between the intent and the deed as far as his righteousness was concerned. His thinking had not arrived at the conflict between intent and deed which Paul describes in Romans 7:15-19.

In two cases righteousness is related to faith in God. Because of their uniqueness in the Old Testament and because of their being used in the New Testament, these require our special attention. The first is Genesis 15:6, "And he [Abram] believed the LORD; and he reckoned it to him as righteousness"; and the second is Habakkuk 2:4, "but the righteous shall live by his faith."

The setting of the first narrates the promise of countless descendants to Abram when he was still without offspring. The LORD brought him out under the heavens at night to number the stars to demonstrate that Abram's descendants would be beyond number. Because of his childlessness Abram had proposed to resort to the common custom of adopting his chief slave, Eliezer of Damascus, who would become his heir and the propagator of his clan. In this vision the LORD told Abram to abandon that plan and to accept the promise of countless offspring as numberless as the stars. In response Abram dismissed his humanly devised plan and accepted the divinely announced promise. This response of faith in the divine word was reckoned to him as righteousness.

100

The verb "reckon" has a declarative function to indicate what is acceptable in the relationship with the LORD. To declare, therefore, that this act of faith was righteousness indicated that trust in God was a fundamental requisite for fellowship with him. Faith, then, as well as delight in the law, is an attitude of heart which characterizes the righteous who live in relationship with God.

The second reference appears in the setting of the prophet Habakkuk's complaint about the prosperity of the wicked. He had seen violence and wrong within Judah; the law was so weak that justice could not prevail. The prophet was told that the LORD was arousing the Chaldean power to execute justice upon the wickedness of Judah. Although the prophet saw this just retribution take place, he was perplexed by an even greater problem, for he saw that the wicked Chaldean swallowed up a people more righteous than he. This proud power of Babylon spurned God and worshipped implements of warfare. Thus the prophet wished to learn what the LORD would answer concerning his complaint. He was told to wait and see that God would finally act to vindicate the right, for the haughty power of evil would fall, but the righteous shall live by his faith. The righteous, in this case the prophet, is the member of the community of God's people who ought to be characterized by faith. In this context faith can either be interpreted as trust in God's eventual prevailing justice and triumph over evil, or as faithfulness or steadfastness in his calling to be a prophet in the midst of perplexity. In both interpretations we observe that the prophet was told that the righteous man demonstrates faith in God who will surely act to bring justice.

In summary, righteousness is ascribed to those who keep the commands of the LORD, who go beyond the literal requirements of the law, and who find delight in the study of the law and willingly obey it, for the law was not regarded as burdensome, but a practical and possible way of life by which the righteous could walk (**cf.** Deut. 30:11-14). Finally, the righteous man manifests faith in the promise of God; moreover, he will have an attitude of trust in God whose sovereign rule in the world shall ultimately cause right to prevail. The righteous man, therefore, performs those deeds, and possesses those attitudes of heart, which constitute the norms by which the covenant community lives.

The Righteousness of the LORD

The above survey of righteousness establishes its importance in God's covenant with Israel. Since the LORD placed Israel in the covenant it would naturally follow that his righteousness would reflect his covenantal love. If we seek a norm by which to understand righteousness then it must be the covenant which God established.

The deliverance from Egypt, which was the prelude for establishing the covenant, and the deliverances or triumphs of Israel from the time of the wilderness wandering to the time of the Judges are designated as the righteousnesses, *sideqoth,* of

102

the LORD. When Israel desired a king, Samuel rehearsed these righteousnesses which began when the LORD sent Moses and Aaron to bring Israel out of Egypt, and which continued during the period of the Judges who delivered Israel from her oppressors (I Sam. 12:6-11). Micah spoke of the deliverances from Egypt and from the devices of Balak king of Moab until Israel arrived in Gilgal as the righteousnesses of the LORD (6:4-5; cf. also the song of Deborah, Judg. 5:11, and Ps. 103:6-7). These references will suffice to show that God acted in righteousness to place Israel within the covenant, and that he continued to manifest his righteousness to Israel within the covenant by giving her victory over those attacking her and deliverance from her oppressors.

Righteousness also embraces concepts of God as judge. In the enthronement psalms (96-99), the LORD appears as king and judge. He comes to judge the world in righteousness (Ps. 96:13; 98:9). In Israel the judge, *shophet*, was to interpret the law and pronounce judgment or justice, *mishpat*. The throne of the LORD is set upon righteousness and justice (97:2; 89:14). In these psalms righteousness appears in the context of a royal court in which terminologies such as "justice," "equity," and "faithfulness" are employed. From this we should observe, therefore, that as a judge exercises a two-fold capacity to deliver the oppressed and punish the oppressor, so also the LORD in his righteousness manifests a two-fold function: deliverance on the one hand and punishment on the other. Although some scholars assert that no puni-

103

tive factor can be seen in righteousness, for punishment is related to the wrath of God,[3] the intimate association of righteousness with court language would imply something of a punitive quality. The deliverance of Israel from her foes has as its counterpart the destruction of her enemies.

The penal element in righteousness takes on clearer expression in Isaiah where, in describing the deliverance of the oppressed and the destruction of the wicked, the prophet declares that the LORD thus shows himself in justice and righteousness (5:13-17; 1:27-28). The destruction decreed for Israel will overflow with righteousness (10:22). Those who have made lies their refuge and falsehood their shelter shall know that justice and righteousness shall destroy all protective devices of the wicked (28:15-17). It must be admitted, however, that righteousness is primarily related to the bringing of deliverance and the maintaining of proper covenantal relationships, and that punishment and destruction are more commonly related to the wrath of the LORD than to his righteousness.

Other prophets like Hosea speak about the LORD's coming to restore Israel to himself in righteousness and justice, in steadfast love, in faithfulness, and in mercy (2:21-22 [19-20]). The description of the messianic prince in Isaiah pictures the great deliverer who shall establish and uphold the throne of David with justice and righteousness (9:6 [7]); and with righteousness as the girdle of his waist he shall deliver the poor and the meek (11:4-5). Jeremiah also speaks of the coming of the righteous Branch who will bring salvation and security to Judah and Israel, and who carries the meaningful name "the LORD is our righteousness" (23:5-6).

Righteousness as salvation and redemption comes to fullest expression in Deutero-Isaiah. This prophet related righteousness to the restoration of the covenant people to their homeland. Covenantal language, such as "steadfast love," "faithfulness," and "salvation," is identified with righteousness to describe the acts of the LORD who is about to deliver Israel from her wearisome exile: "My righteousness draws near speedily, my salvation has gone forth . . . my salvation will be for ever, and my righteousness will never be ended" (Is. 51:5-6) Cyrus, whose right hand the LORD has grasped to subdue nations before him, has been aroused in righteousness that he may set the exiles free and build their city (45:1,13). The prospect of using Cyrus, the pagan prince, for Israel's salvation issues into a hymn of exaltation which celebrates the wonder of the LORD's righteousness:

> Shower, O heavens, from above,
> and let the skies rain down righteousness;
> let the earth open, that salvation may sprout forth,
> and let it cause righteousness to spring up also;
> I the LORD have created it (45:8).

Righteousness extends its meaning to victory over foes, as seen in the stirring up of one from the east, Cyrus, whom righteousness (victory, thus R.S.V., also New Dutch and Zürich versions) meets at every step. Here as before we encounter the double function of righteousness, which brings salva-

105

tion and deliverance for the oppressed and defeat to the oppressor. Victory may well have the sense of righteousness (41:10) where the LORD will uphold Israel with the right hand of his victory, or with his victorious right hand (thus R.S.V. and Zürich).

The wonder of this righteousness is that it takes on universal dimensions which will come to fruition through the giving of the Servant as the covenant for Israel and for the nations (42:6-7; 45:22-23; 51:4-5). The covenant relationship now reaches beyond the borders of Israel to incorporate all creatures of the Creator. Here the divine righteousness consummates the covenant's original purpose to bring in the nations even as Israel was brought in through redemptive grace. This extension of righteousness results not from Israel's efforts but from a renewed manifestation of the LORD's righteousness.

Those of us who have inherited the conventional understanding of righteousness cannot but be greatly impressed and indeed surprised with the meaning of righteousness as given so succinctly by the prophet of the exile: "And there is no other god besides me, a righteous God and a Savior; there is none besides me" (45:21). A. B. Davidson makes a revealing comment about this passage: "The antithesis which in dogmatics we are familiar with is a righteous or just God and *yet* a Saviour. The Old Testament puts it differently—a righteous God, and *therefore* a Saviour."[4]

The psalmists, who also use covenantal language, give righteousness the sense of salvation and deliverance. In his prayer for vindication because of those who hate him without cause the psalmist appeals to the LORD's righteousness (Ps. 35:24, 28). Deliverance from fears within and foes without is described in terms of the covenantal vocabulary of "salvation," "mercy," "faithfulness," and "steadfast love" among which "righteousness" takes a prominent place (40:10-11 [9-10]; 85:11-12 [10-11]). In his praise for deliverance the psalmist will greatly magnify the LORD's righteousness (71:15-16, 19, 24). So closely is righteousness associated with deliverance that the psalmist's prayer of imprecation implores that his foes may not come into God's righteousness, but that punishment may continue (69:28 [27]). In the past the LORD performed his righteousness for his people Israel in delivering them, and he continues his covenantal steadfast love and righteousness from generation to generation (103:6, 17-18). In his gratitude at being restored into the covenantal fellowship from which his sin and guilt had barred him the psalmist addresses his praise to the righteousness of God for deliverance from guilt, which in effect relates righteousness to the pardoning grace of God (51:16 [14]; cf. 143:1-12, and Mic. 7:9, 18-20, in which covenantal terminologies including "righteousness" are used to describe God in his pardoning of iniquity and his passing over transgression).

From our survey of the Old Testament data on righteousness we can observe that we do not have a *iustitia distributiva*, a righteousness by which God dispenses rewards and punishments according to some ethical norm, but rather a *iustitia*

107

salutifera, a righteousness by which he promotes his covenant purpose to bring salvation to Israel and ultimately to the nations. Righteousness consists of the living quality within God that transcends all standards of morals and laws, for in his righteousness God can and does deliver and restore Israel and the nations, who because of their transgressions are unable to deliver and restore themselves. This unique and praise-provoking manifestation of the LORD's righteousness produces a profound effect upon all who receive it, for they, as the righteous in the covenant, will demonstrate their righteousness by a willing self-dedication in service to bring deliverance and restoration to the needy and afflicted who are unable to help themselves.

Righteousness at Qumran and Among the Apocalyptists

At Qumran the term righteousness of God takes an important place in the writings of the sect. It is used parallel with the steadfast loves (plural of *ḥesedh*) of God: "And when I stumble the steadfast loves of God are always my salvation; and when I stagger because of the evil of my flesh my right shall forever stand through the righteousness of God" *(Manual of Discipline* 11:12). In the quoted work, righteousness has a double function in that through it God offers his help to his faithful people and readily pardons their transgressions. In his righteousness God is also faithful to his new creation, the holy community. In passing, it is note-

108

worthy that the singular form of "righteousness" is used in contrast to the plural form *sideqoth* which, with one exception (Deut. 33:21), appears in the Old Testament. This usage of the singular may reflect a process of theological abstraction which results in a technical term. This term then takes on the essential meaning of activity in salvation history which extends to include his creation and rule of the world.

In the *Thanksgiving Psalm* the righteousness of God manifests covenantal faithfulness to the community at Qumran which God has created and which he has placed in a service of obedience. The obedience and prayer of the community are less its endeavors to place itself in the right before God, and more the manifestation of God's power through the pious by whom God is honored. Further, in righteousness God is ready to forgive transgressions and to lead the community into the blessed end time. In all these manifestations of salvation it is God's righteousness and not human power that must be recognized.

The apocalyptic language of *The War of the Children of Light Against the Children of Darkness* would naturally present the righteousness of God in terms of warfare, of judgment, and of bringing the community into the full realization of salvation. The holy war follows a course of judgment and vindication in which the holy community shall eventually possess God's complete salvation and deliverance.

In summary, the Qumran writings use the righteousness of God as a technical term also found in Judaistic apocalypticism of that time. Essentially it means the covenantal faithfulness of God which is being revealed especially in the eschatological warfare for the rule of God's justice. The humble and the penitent shall experience this action of God as the foundation of their righteousness. In the holy war the members of the community will maintain this righteousness by their obedience to the law as interpreted by the teacher of righteousness. The righteousness of God in its eschatological perspective takes hold of the present age and reaches into the future age to consummate the rule of God. All this in effect states that righteousness is the advent of God to establish his reign over the world which he has created for his glory.

In the apocalyptic writings of Judaism such as *The Book of Enoch, The Jubilees, The Testaments of the Twelve Patriarchs,* and others, the righteousness of God has much the same usage as at Qumran. It includes the concepts of God's faithfulness to his covenant people, his just rule over all creation, and his compassionate forgiveness. Because of the chaotic conditions and often because of the oppression in which the people of God found themselves, questions were raised about the dependability of God's justice, about his covenantal faithfulness, and about his rule in the world he had created. As seers and visionaries addressed themselves to these problems, they wrote of the righteousness of God as the basic assurance that God's rule would prevail, either in the immediate future or in the more distant time.

110

Righteousness in the New Testament

In the Gospel of Matthew righteousness carries a significant theological meaning which has obvious Old Testament background.[5] The key verse for the understanding of righteousness is, "seek first his kingdom and his righteousness [*dikaiosunê*], and all these things shall be yours as well" (6:33). Righteousness and kingdom are here combined and related to God as the pronoun "his" indicates (cf. ver. 32). Matthew brings the covenant people of the Old Testament and the relationships of righteousness God demonstrated toward his people into view as background. Righteousness, which here sets the goal for the attitude and conduct of believers, must therefore be understood in the light of God's kingdom and the relationships within that kingdom. The righteousness of the disciple need not be identical with God's righteousness, but it should correspond to that of God (cf. 5:48).

In the beatitudes the ones who hunger and thirst for righteousness (5:6) are those whose interests are manifested in making evident the righteousness of God as seen in his acts of deliverance of the oppressed, in his forgiveness for the transgressor, and in his faithfulness to his people. The zeal to demonstrate this kind of conduct may result in persecution (5:10). The first reference, which has in mind the righteousness of God, and the second reference, which describes human manifestation of righteousness, are brought together in verse 11 with "on my account," thereby describing the

111

christological nature of the kingdom which Jesus had proclaimed and had established. Thus, the perplexing problem of being persecuted and being falsely accused takes on meaning in the light of the suffering and death of Christ.

The righteousness of the disciples was to be of a higher quality than that of the scribes and Pharisees: "For I tell you, unless your righteousness exceeds that of the scribes and Pharisees, you will never enter the kingdom of heaven" (5:20). Here also righteousness and kingdom are combined and this indicates that Jesus is speaking about conduct that should characterize living within that kingdom. During the intertestamental period we can detect a tendency to regard righteousness as synonymous with giving of alms since the LXX in fourteen instances translates the Hebrew *ṣedheq* with *eleêmosunê,* giving alms. The close association of righteousness with deeds of mercy may be seen in Daniel 4:24 [27], "Therefore, O king, let my counsel be accepted to you; break off your sins by practicing righteousness, and your iniquities by showing mercy to the oppressed, that there may perhaps be a lengthening of your tranquility" (**cf.** also Ecclesiasticus 7:10; 29:12; Tobit 4:10; 12:9). The better reading for Matthew 6:1 has *dikaiosunê.* "Beware of doing your righteousness before men," a word changed to *eleêmosunê* in later manuscripts and thus made to agree with the context of the following verses. As we have observed, righteousness in the Old Testament has to do with kindness and compassion for the oppressed, for proper relationships within the covenant are thus maintained. So also, in the kingdom of heaven about which Jesus spoke, righteousness as expressed in attitudes of love and in deeds of compassion becomes the prime requirement for entering and living in that kingdom. Similarly in the description of the eschatological kingdom at the end of the age those who have shown concern for the hungry, the afflicted, and the lonely are called the righteous who enter eternal life (25:46). And when all offenses and evildoers have been removed, then "the righteous will shine like the sun in the kingdom of their Father" (13:43).

Righteousness receives its most detailed exposition in the New Testament at the hands of the Apostle Paul. Many scholars, both ancient and modern, have given extensive study to this important subject in Paul's thought. To undertake a survey of all that has been written on this phase of the Apostle's writing would require space and time beyond the purpose of this chapter. For our purposes it will suffice to discuss a few important passages on righteousness from which we can acquire Paul's understanding of that term, especially as it relates to Old Testament thought.

Romans 1:16-17 is primary for our consideration.

> For I am not ashamed of the gospel: it is the power of God for salvation to every one who has faith, to the Jew first and also to the Greek. For in it the righteousness of God is revealed through faith for faith; as it is written, "He who through faith is righteous shall live."

113

In announcing his theme by declaring that he is not ashamed of the gospel Paul makes known his confession of faith in which he states his understanding of the gospel. This gospel is first of all the power of God to bring about salvation; and secondly, as though to answer a proposed question how one may know that the gospel has salvation power, Paul asserts that the righteousness of God is revealed in this gospel. Paul has here taken over from the Old Testament the concepts of redemption and deliverance which are incorporated in the righteousness of God, especially as proclaimed by the prophet of the exile. We may assume that the readers of this epistle knew the Old Testament meaning of righteousness so that its use served to help them understand the salvation power of the gospel.

In the introduction to this epistle Paul recalled that he had been set apart for the gospel of God which had been promised beforehand by the prophets and which had now taken place in the coming of his Son, Jesus Christ, who was designated the Son of God by his resurrection from the dead (1:1-4). Paul observed that the promised salvation of the prophets was now being revealed through the gospel. In line with that promise he used the Old Testament word "righteousness" so that the reader could make no mistake in knowing that the God of Israel who in righteousness had delivered his people, especially from the Babylonian exile, had now also come in righteousness to accomplish salvation.

In stating that righteousness was revealed Paul

114

made clear the supernatural aspect of the gospel, an aspect which also applied to the righteous acts of the LORD in the Old Testament. We should note, however, that the revelation of righteousness was more than a vision or spiritual communication to a prophet for it took place in the events of time. As Deutero-Isaiah spoke of the coming deliverance of his day he declared that God's righteousness would be seen in events such as the coming of Cyrus, the destruction of Babylon, and the return of the exiles to their homeland. The redemption of Israel took place on the stage of history where all flesh could see the salvation of God (Is. 40:5; 52:10). The revelation of the gospel was likewise an event in history in the person of Jesus of Nazareth whose life and death had been observed by those of his generation. Thus it can be seen that the righteousness revealed in the gospel had the same dimension in history which was evident in the righteousness of God in the Old Testament.

One cannot but be impressed by the emphasis which Paul places on faith in this passage "to every one who has faith," "revealed through faith for faith," and "he who through faith is righteous shall live." It becomes clear that faith is the God-given and -ordained means by which righteousness becomes the possession of the believer. In the preaching of Deutero-Isaiah Paul found the word "righteousness" abundantly, but he would not find "faith," except by implication, in such passages which speak about those waiting for the LORD (40:31) or about turning to the LORD to be saved (45:22; cf. also 55:1-3). For the word "faith" and

115

its special significance Paul reached beyond the prophet to Abraham (Rom. 4) and to the prophet Habakkuk: "But the righteous shall live by his faith" (Hab. 2:4).

His use of Abraham as found in Genesis, "And he believed the LORD; and he reckoned it to him as righteousness" (15:6), became the important argument with the Jews to show that their forefather was righteous because of faith and not because of his keeping the law. Abraham believed that God would do what he had promised, and because of his faith he was declared to be righteous, which is to say that he was in proper relationship with God. This meant that before he could have performed any demand of the law or rite of the covenant Abraham had righteousness through faith (Rom. 4:9-11). This then does away with any righteousness through the law, for Abraham set the example of righteousness through faith.

Based on his concept of the righteousness of Abraham, Paul also developed the argument for the universalism of the gospel. Since Abraham had that righteousness before his circumcision while he was still a Gentile, he indeed becomes the father of all who believe without being circumcised, as well as of all who are circumcised and believe. For Paul it was clear that in the Old Testament at the very beginning of redemption history Abraham's righteousness through faith had as its goal the wide sweep of universalism. That particular goal had been fully achieved in the gospel of God which is for every one who has faith, whether Jew or Greek. The universal dimensions of the gospel, therefore, are already to be found in the righteousness of Abraham, who has become "the father of all who believe without being circumcised and who thus have righteousness reckoned to them" (4:11).

The usage of "the righteousness of God" in the Old Testament and its usage in Romans may be observed in the following passage:

> For there is no distinction; since all have sinned and fall short of the glory of God, they are justified by his grace as a gift, through the redemption which is in Christ Jesus, whom God put forward as an expiation by his blood, to be received by faith. This was to show God's righteousness, because in his divine forbearance he had passed over former sins; it was to prove at the present time that he himself is righteous and that he justifies him who has faith in Jesus (3:22b-26).

In the preceding section of this epistle (1:18-3:20) Paul has described the fallen world which is under the wrath of God. The creature has rebelled against the Creator to bring all mankind under wrath. The coming of the law, which was indeed of great value and advantage to the Jew (3:1-2), did not remove the judgment of God upon the world, for the law could not deliver, but merely gave the knowledge of sin (3:20). Paul's use of the phrase "but now," the introductory words for the new section (3:21-26), intends to set the righteousness of God, introduced in the theme of the epistle (1:16-17), over against the wrath of God. The darkness and doom of wrath is the background against which the light of the righteousness of God shines. Thus Paul means to declare how mankind, sinful and falling short of the "glory of God" (3:23), a term synonymous with the "righteousness of God," has been redeemed through that righteousness manifested in Jesus Christ.

In this passage, Paul proposes to explicate the righteousness of God in its manifestation (ver. 25-26, *endeixis*) in the former time, which included the Old Testament, and in the present time, the new age of the gospel of God.

Paul has already noted that the law was given in the former time, yet there was no righteousness through the works of the law, that is, through observance of the legal code; nonetheless, the law and the prophets, that is, the Old Testament, bear witness to the righteousness of God (3:21; 4:3). In what way did the Old Testament show the righteousness of God as it pertained to sins committed during that time? Paul asks. He answers, in the light of the redemption which came into reality in Jesus Christ whom God set forth as the expiation for sin. God thus passed over, or in effect forgave, the sins committed in former times. In passing over these sins God manifested his patience (3:25, *anochê*), or his faithfulness (3:3-4, *pistis*), in contrast to Israel's faithlessness. The point that we should clearly see is that through his forgiving patience God manifested his righteousness in former times.

In the present time the manifestation of the righteousness of God has been revealed in the gospel of God as Paul set it forth (1:16-17). This manifestation, Paul asserts, presents God as being "righteous and making one righteous by faith in Jesus" *(dikaion kai dikaiounta ton ek pisteôs Iêsou).*

118

As the righteous one, God here manifests himself as Savior and Redeemer, and as the one making another righteous he declares the believer in Jesus righteous, that is, in proper relationship with God. Paul could speak about God as both being righteous and making sinful man righteous (cf. 4:5) without regarding it as a paradox, although, as C. H. Dodd observes, many of Paul's interpreters have done so.[6] Although the Greek or classical meaning of righteousness as a moral standard, which is indeed our common understanding of righteousness, was known to Paul, yet he was firmly committed to the usage of righteousness found in the law and the prophets. In that "law" Paul learned that Abraham was reckoned righteous because he believed God's promise (Gen. 15:6), and in the prophets he had read, "a righteous God and a Savior" (Is. 45:21).

The background to Paul's polemic against the idea of righteousness by works of the law indicates a growth of appreciation for the law and its special significance in Judaism. Judaism found the origin for this high evaluation of the law in the Old Testament. We have noted above that in certain psalms which celebrate the excellence of the law (Pss. 1, 19, 119) the righteous ones delight in the law and meditate on it constantly. The law has become for them the way of life which they realize in keeping the commandments. Furthermore the commandments were not impossible to keep (Deut. 30:11,14). In Ezekiel's sermon on individual responsibility to be demonstrated in the daily requirements of living the prophet declares that the

119

one keeping the commandments is righteous, and he shall surely live in the congregation of Israel (Ezek. 18:9). We also observed in Deuteronomy that the careful keeping of the commandments would be Israel's righteousness (6:25; 24:13). Deutero-Isaiah speaks about righteousness which results from feeding the poor and befriending the needy (Is. 58:7-10). But from this high evaluation of the law Judaism developed a legalism that produced a meritorious righteousness through the works of the law. This was the kind of righteousness Paul had achieved: "As to the law a Pharisee, as to zeal a persecutor of the church, as to righteousness under the law blameless" (Phil. 3:5b-6).

Paul, who on the one hand had great respect and concern for his fellow Jews and on the other hand had learned that Judaism's zeal for God was not enlightened (Rom. 10:1-3), formally states the issue on righteousness which marks the boundary between Paul as a Jew and Paul as a Christian: "That I may gain Christ and be found in him, not having a righteousness of my own based on law, but that which is through faith in Christ, the righteousness from God that depends on faith" (Phil. 3:8b-9). The Greek text clearly distinguishes between righteousness from the law or righteousness from God. The righteousness from God which was manifested in Christ was of such excellence that all righteousness from the law faded into worthlessness. This excellence which appears in the righteousness from God makes possible the knowledge of Christ and the power of his resurrection (3:10). This is to say that in "knowing Christ Jesus" (ver.

8) Paul experienced the power of Christ's resurrection which placed him in a new life as the sacrament of baptism symbolized (Rom. 6:3-11). We, therefore, can discern that the righteousness from God brings a salvation that reaches its consummation in the resurrection of Christ. Thus righteousness embraces resurrection, the power which brings life out of death. This kind of righteousness was abundantly manifested in the history of Israel, for in his righteousness (or his righteous acts) God brought Israel out of the death of Egypt; he further preserved her from being swallowed up in the death of Canaanite culture and idolatry; and in his final demonstration of righteousness God delivered his people from the death of Babylonian exile. Paul could thus affirm in truth that the Old Testament bears witness to the righteousness of God (Rom. 3:21). His acceptance of that righteousness acknowledges that the Old Testament witness of God's redemptive acts has been fully consummated in the resurrection of Christ in which Paul and all believers may participate.[7]

Since in his epistle James makes a significant appeal to the righteousness which was reckoned to Abraham, we should examine his use of that term.

The first mention of righteousness by James is to contrast the righteousness of God with the anger of men, "for the anger of man does not work the righteousness of God" (1:20). James is urging his readers to suppress anger, for it will not produce that which characterizes the righteousness of God.

121

Righteousness here carries the meaning found in Matthew: almsgiving, readiness to forgive, faithfulness, and compassion for the oppressed. In manifesting righteousness rather than anger Christians could show that they were a kind of first fruits of God's creatures (1:18).

James' second mention of righteousness has to do with the reference to Abraham (Gen. 15:6): "Abraham believed God, and it was reckoned to him as righteousness" (2:23). James here associates righteousness with the obedience of Abraham in offering his son Isaac on the altar (Gen. 22), an association also made by the writer in I Maccabees 2:52. Paul's use of this reference, however, as discussed above, was to emphasize that righteousness was not achieved by works of the law, for righteousness was reckoned to Abraham because he believed in God's promise. James' thesis is that righteousness was accounted to Abraham because of his obedience to the divine command to sacrifice Isaac.

The obvious difference in the two writers' perception of the manner in which righteousness was reckoned to Abraham—in the case of James through obedience, in the case of Paul through faith—can be explained in a large measure by a clear understanding of what each author means when he uses the words "faith" and "works." In Paul's use of faith, *pistis,* he means a complete reliance on God, whereas James intends it to be an intellectual assent to monotheism (2:19). To Paul, works, *erga,* would be the observing of the ceremonial law such as circumcision, but to James they

122

are deeds of love such as providing for the needy (2:15-16). In no case does James associate works with the keeping of the ceremonial law. Moreover, James is presupposing the presence of faith which must express itself in works of love. Paul would agree to this as he expresses it in his eloquent description of love (I Cor. 13:2).

In his contention for righteousness through faith Paul is battling against confidence in meritorious works, against an underestimation of sin, and against a spirit of self-righteousness. He would underscore Jesus' teaching about being poor in spirit and humble of heart (cf. Mt. 5:3-6; Lk. 18:14). James, also in harmony with Jesus' teaching about being doers of God's will, is contending against dead orthodoxy (cf. Mt. 7:21-23). The difference between Paul's conception of righteousness through faith without works, and James' conception of righteousness through doing God's command is not fully resolved, but is greatly clarified as we take into account the *Sitz im Leben* of each author and the consequent meaning each one attaches to the words "faith" and "works."[8]

Summary

A summary on righteousness may appropriately call attention to three main concepts that explicate the term in the Scriptures.

1. Righteousness as manifested by God is seen in his mighty acts of deliverance. These began in bringing Israel out of the Egyptian bondage, they continued in Israel's history, and they were es-

pecially seen in Israel's restoration from Babylonian exile. This concept of deliverance came to consummate fulfillment in the gospel as demonstrated through the death and resurrection of Jesus Christ. Thus Paul declared that the gospel is the power of God for salvation, "for in it the righteousness of God is revealed through faith for faith" (Rom. 1:17).

2. Righteousness is intimately related to faith as seen in the case of Abraham to whom righteousness was reckoned because he believed. Here Paul found his primary example to declare that righteousness was not to be acquired through works but through faith in Jesus Christ.

3. Righteousness is a quality or characteristic of the righteous in Israel who faithfully kept the law which was their special delight. Even though the keeping of the law did lead to a legalism that promoted self-esteem, yet even in the New Testament righteousness was to be expressed in deeds of charity, compassion, and obedience to God's will.

NOTES

1. H. Cazelles, "A propos de quelques textes difficiles relatifs a la justice de Dieu dans l'A.T.," *Revue Biblique* (1951), pp. 169 ff.

2. E. Kautzsch, *Die Derivate des Stammes sdq im alttestamentlichen Sprachgebrauch* (Tübingen, 1881).

3. G. von Rad, *Old Testament Theology*, Vol. I (New York: Harper & Brothers, 1962), p. 377; **cf.** E.

Jacob's criticism of "non-punitive" righteousness, *Theology of the Old Testament* (New York: Harper & Brothers, 1958), pp. 99-100; also L. J. Kuyper, *The Righteousness of God in the Old Testament* (Holland, Michigan: Western Theological Seminary, 1943), pp. 13-15.

4. A. B. Davidson, *The Theology of the Old Testament* (Edinburgh: T. & T. Clark, 1904), p. 144.

5. P. Stuhlmacher, *Gerechtigkeit Gottes bei Paulus* (Göttingen: Vandenhoeck & Ruprecht, 1965), pp. 188-91.

6. C. H. Dodd, *The Bible and the Greeks* (London: Hodder & Stoughton, 1954), p. 57; cf. further Dodd's discussion of the paradox and his exposition of Romans 3:25-26, *The Epistle of Paul to the Romans* (London: Collins Clear-type Press, 1959), pp. 76-84.

7. Recommended Studies of Paul's Exposition of the Righteousness of God: C. K. Barrett, *The Epistle to the Romans* (London: Adam & Charles Black, 1957), pp. 71-84; A. Nygren, *Commentary on Romans* (Philadelphia: Muhlenberg Press, 1949), pp. 144-84; J. H. Ropes, " 'Righteousness' and 'The Righteousness of God' in the Old Testament and in St. Paul," *Journal of Biblical Literature*, Vol. 22 (1903), pp. 221-27; G. Schrenk, *Theological Dictionary of the New Testament*, Vol. II (Grand Rapids: Wm. B. Eerdmans Publishing Co., 1964), pp. 202-10; P. Stuhlmacher, *op. cit.*, pp. 74-101.

8. M. Dibelius offers a summary maxim about the Paul-James issue on faith-works: "The faith of Abraham helped his works, and the works perfected his faith." In James' thought the completion of this faith arrived at something higher, a goal for both faith and works, which is Abraham's righteousness; *Der Brief des Jakobus* (Göttingen: Vandenhoeck & Ruprecht, 1959), pp. 152-53. B. Reicke lessens the Paul-James tension in observing that James views man's justification (righteousness)

with the final judgment in mind, whereas Paul has the believer's conversion and baptism in mind; *The Epistles of James, Peter, and Jude,* The Anchor Bible (Garden City, New York: Doubleday & Company, Inc., 1964), pp. 34-35. Other recommended studies: J. Jeremias, "Paul and James," *The Expository Times* (September, 1955), pp. 368-71; J. Moffatt, *The General Epistles,* The Moffatt New Testament Commentary (Garden City, New York: Doubleday, Doran & Company, 1928), pp. 42-45; P. Stuhlmacher, *op. cit.,* pp. 191-94.

CHAPTER V

THE HOLY ONE OF ISRAEL AND THE HOLY SPIRIT

HOLINESS PLAYS AN IMPORTANT ROLE IN THE account of the LORD's relationship with Israel. More than any other descriptive words including "love," "wrath," or "righteousness," "holiness" and "holy" are identified with the LORD, so that "The Holy One" becomes a divine name. God is not only called *Qadôsh*, The Holy One (Is. 40:25), or The Holy One of Israel (41:14,20), but his name itself is declared to be *Qadosh* (Ps. 111:9). Praise is ascribed to *shem qadeshô*, the name of his holiness (Ps. 103:1). "Holy" was so firmly attached to the divine name that Judaism still uses the name Holy One in its liturgy and Christians designate the third person of the Trinity as the Holy Spirit, the significance of which will appear later in this chapter.

The root derivation of holiness, *QDSH*, cannot be determined with certainty. It seems likely that its origin in Canaanite sources may be found in the root *QD*, "to separate," which suggests the idea of a separation from the common and ordinary. Some scholars suggest that the word stems from Arabic or Assyrian backgrounds which offer the meaning "to be pure or bright," but Eichrodt

127

regards this as a derived meaning from a root whose original meaning is unknown.[1] We do well to remember that it is the Old Testament that gives holiness its primary classical meaning of separation from the common and profane for sacred purposes.

The primary sense of holiness as ascribed to God embraced the concepts of exaltedness and transcendence. In the vision of Isaiah (ch. 6) the prophet saw the Lord seated on a throne high and lifted up and not enthroned upon the cherubim above the ark (Ps. 80:2 [1]; 99:1). So also Deutero-Isaiah spoke about God dwelling in the high and holy place (Is. 57:15), or in the heaven above (63:15; cf. also Ps. 11:4; 20:7 [6]; 102:20 [19]). The descriptive synonyms for "holiness" are "terribleness," "majesty," and "wonder." "Glory," *kabod,* as seen in the prophet's vision, was frequently associated with holiness to suggest the external brilliance of the exalted holiness. This glory had something of a cosmic quality which filled the earth, whereas holiness reflected the personal being of God in relationship to mankind and the world.

The transcendence of holiness established the unapproachability of God, so that Moses was told to remove his shoes from his feet because he was standing on holy ground (Ex. 3:5), and Israel was to be kept away from the holy mount (19:21-24). The ceremonial laws which kept the common or profane from contact with the sacred took this unapproachability into account. This separation, a religious phenomenon that emphasized the difference between God and the people, took on ethical and moral dimensions in the vision of Isaiah who became aware of his sin and the sin of his people. We should not limit the unapproachability of holiness to ethical or moral factors as is commonly done, for this unapproachability also accentuates the mysterious exaltedness of the divine over against human weakness and finiteness. Although some are wont to dub ceremonial restriction in matters of worship another form of tabu so common in primitive and natural religions, we ought not to denigrate the cultic elements of holiness, for they established the much needed distinction between God and man, without which even the Christian faith can be reduced to a mere cultural manifestation in the world.

By properly defining holiness as inherent in God rather than in the objects or personnel of the cult, we mark out the primary distinction between the Old Testament and the religions of Canaan. Yet it must be conceded that, like her neighbors, Israel had holy objects, places, and personnel. This type of holiness should be regarded as derived from the LORD. It may be that a place became holy because of a theophany, as at Sinai (Ex. 3:5;19:10-14) or at Jericho (Josh. 5:15). When the LORD led the people of Israel out of Egypt to establish a covenant with them, they became a "holy nation" (Ex. 19:6), which meant that God had bestowed holiness upon them. They had been delivered from the Egyptian bondage to become God's possession in the relationship of the covenant. In this relationship they received holiness. The ark of the LORD, more than any other object, was considered holy because it contained the law given by God to Israel; the LORD sat above this ark upon an invisible throne which accounts for the liturgical address, "Thou who art enthroned upon the cherubim." Although the ark was recklessly and superstitiously used in the battles with the Philistines (I Sam. 4-6), a use which clearly demonstrated how easily a consecrated object could become identified with deity, yet the people of Bethshemesh recognized not the ark but the LORD: "Who is able to stand before the LORD, this holy God?" (I Sam. 6:20). This confession took account of the presence of God in his holiness rather than of an impersonal power within a sacred object.

Holiness, as a quality given by the LORD and as an indication of a special relationship with him, was ascribed to the sabbath (Gen. 2:3; Ex. 20:8,11); to the garments worn by the priests (Ex. 28:1-4); to the altar, the tent, and the priests (29:37,44); to the anointing oil which transferred holiness on the object or person anointed (30:22-33); to the specially prepared incense (30:34-38); to different offerings (Lev. 6:17,25,29; 7:6); and to the tithe (Deut. 26:12-13).[2] Cultic objects and persons stood in a special relationship to the LORD from whom they received the state or quality of holiness.

Our understanding of the above forms of cultic holiness should, on the one hand, make plain that these were not concerned with moral conduct or ethical standards, and, on the other hand, should indicate that in her observance of cultic laws Israel was responding to a personal being who, although exalted and lifted up, was calling Israel into a fellowship of holiness that bridged the mystery or chasm between God and man. In her best use of cultic holiness Israel took note that the majestic and sovereign God, both at Mt. Sinai and at Mt. Zion, had come into a redemptive fellowship which preserved his transcendence, his complete otherness, and his nearness through the cult. However, in her misuse of the cult Israel degraded the holiness of worship to a crass manipulation of forms and rites, thereby reducing the God of holiness to an impersonal force that dispensed favors and prosperity. Jeremiah protested against this misuse, warning of deception behind the words, "This is the temple of the LORD, the temple of the LORD, the temple of the LORD" (Jer. 7:4). The holy place had in fact become a den for robbers.

The ethical, however, was not obliterated out of the predominate place that holiness had in the history of Israel. The priestly legislation of the Pentateuch maintained a significant emphasis on proper conduct and on consideration for the neighbor. Though the priestly class was preoccupied with temple and cult, an important segment of priests had a passion for the moral rectitude of the people and a compassionate concern for the oppressed even as was manifested by priest-prophets such as Jeremiah and Ezekiel. It is therefore not surprising to find that in the priestly legislation moral laws frequently appear within the context of cultic legislation. The exposition of the text, "You shall be holy, for I the LORD your God am holy" (Lev. 19:2), made clear that moral purity and uprightness were a part of holiness. Parents, for example, were to be honored (ver. 3); the poor were to be remembered in the reaping of the fields and the gathering of grapes (ver. 9-10); deceit and theft were forbidden (ver. 11-12); oppression, injustice, partial judgment, and slander were prohibited (ver. 13-16); neither hate nor revenge, but love toward the neighbor was enjoined (ver. 17-18); strangers were not to be wronged (ver. 35-36); and adultery and lust were strongly condemned (20:10ff.). Cultic laws and ethical demands were not differentiated in the holiness legislation. Quite naturally this type of legislation seems strange to our modern culture which has lost its religious orientation, for we place high value on moral and ethical demands in life but condone ceremonial or ritual requirements of religious groups as some vestige of a bygone culture that can serve no practical purpose in the common life. Israel, however, knew of no distinction between the ethical and the cultic.

The cultic and the ethical are joined in Psalms 15 and 24 in what have been called "the liturgies of the gate." These psalms picture the worshipping congregation standing before the gate of the temple and asking what the prerequisites are for entering:

> "O LORD, who shall sojourn in thy tent?
> Who shall dwell on thy holy hill?" (15:1; also 24:3).

To these questions the officiating priest would give answer:

He who walks blamelessly, and does what is right
and speaks truth from his heart;
who does not slander with his tongue,
and does no evil to his friend,
nor takes up a reproach against his neighbor
    (15:2-3).

The emphasis on moral conduct in these liturgies is significant. We need not suppose that only those who achieved moral rectitude would be admitted for worship; rather we are informed that repeated use of these liturgies reminded the worshipper that "clean hands and a pure heart" were standards of conduct and attitudes of life which should ever be present in the Israelite. Preparation for fellowship with God therefore was not merely bringing the sacrifice and the tithe, but also the life dedicated to uprightness and personal integrity. "Such is the generation of those who seek him, who seek the face of the God of Jacob" (24:6).

Isaiah

We owe to Isaiah, the son of Amoz, the fullest understanding of the name "Holy," the name par excellence for the LORD, the God of Israel. The call of the prophet, as recorded in chapter 6, took place in the temple, the place of holiness. In his vision the prophet did not see the LORD enthroned upon the cherubim above the holy ark, but on a throne high and lifted up with his royal robes filling the temple. The first impression of the vision emphasized the Lord's exaltedness and transcendence which graphically defined his holiness. This holiness was made especially prominent by

133

the three-fold *Qadosh* of the seraphim who declared that this transcendent holiness had universal dimensions since its glory, *kabhôdh,* the cosmic radiant manifestation of holiness, filled the entire earth. Transcendence and universal glory were the setting in which the prophet saw his own sinful nature and that of his people, for holiness also had the quality of moral purity. The prophet realized that his moral impurity could not exist in the presence of the purity of divine holiness, and therefore cried out, "Woe is me! For I am lost; for I am a man of unclean lips" (6:4). In the cultic expiation performed by one of the seraphim the prophet's sin was forgiven and his fear of annihilation was allayed. Yet the moral impurity of the people remained, as became clear in the commission to him, for their reliance on the ceremonial holiness of the temple cult made them amazingly deaf, blind, and heavy of heart, so that they would not respond to the preaching of the prophet who had seen the moral purity of the LORD's holiness (6:9-12).

The ministry of this commissioned prophet came in the context of the tension drawn between the Holy One of Israel and Israel, the unholy people. The covenant people, who were called a "holy nation" at the time of deliverance from Egypt, had forsaken the LORD and had despised the Holy One of Israel (1:4); they had rejected the law and despised the word of the Holy One (5:24). The sin of Israel was that she had made observance of the cult the standard of holiness and had transgressed all laws for moral living. Because of Israel's rebellion against the moral demands of the law, the divine holiness turned to wrath and declared that judgment awaited a sinful people. Therefore, Sheol, the realm of the dead, like a huge monster had opened wide its mouth to devour the wayward nation (5:13-16).

The wrath of the Holy One possessed a two-fold purpose: (1) Like a fire it would utterly consume and destroy; and (2) it would also cleanse and purify. The holy wrath would burn not only the worthless thorns and briers, but also the glory of the forest and the fruitful land (10:17-18). The destructive calamity would be overwhelming so that only a remnant which a child could number would remain (10:19). However, the remnant would remain and return to the Holy One of Israel in very truth. All this declared that the remnant would then be pure, so that the people would be holy and pure. The holy wrath of God would cleanse his people to set them in a relationship of holiness and purity. This action of God was the background for the apostle Peter's admonition, "but as he who called you is holy, be holy yourselves in all your conduct; since it is written, 'You shall be holy, for I am holy'" (I Pet. 1:15-16).

Isaiah therefore becomes our main source for studying the basic concepts latent in holiness. At the time of his call he encountered the Holy One in his exaltedness, exalted above the holy temple, above the throne of Judah, and above the whole earth. Not cherubim whose forms were set upon the ark in the temple, but living and moving seraphim chanted the Trisagion of praise, thus accentu-

135

ating the transcendence of the LORD Sebaoth. Further, the prophet became aware of God's moral purity in sharp contrast to the moral impurity of the unholy people. The prophet's message then declared that the Holy One would come in wrath to destroy the rebellious people. Holy wrath would also cleanse and purify so that the remnant which would survive the destruction would be pure (10:20-21). This remnant would remain like the stump of a felled oak which would be the holy seed (6:13).

This prophet who had seen the majestic holiness of the LORD and had learned that the glory of that holiness filled all the earth could not but be distressed to observe that his nation sought help from Egypt, and placed confidence in horses and the military power of Egypt, rather than in the Holy One of Israel (30:2-7, 15-16; 31:1). In the oracles against trust in Egypt, the prophet warned against the prophets of illusions and falsehood who turned the people against the word of the Holy One in whom they should have put their trust. However, even among these people who had blind eyes and closed ears (6:9-10), and about whom the prophet had been forewarned, the day would come when the deaf should hear and the blind should see and the meek should rejoice because the Holy One would bring deliverance and salvation (29:18-20). The prophet saw that the sons of Jacob would indeed have a new understanding of confidence in the God who had not only redeemed their forefather Abraham but had also brought redemption to the wayward descendants of Abraham so that they in gratitude would make holy the name of the Holy One of Israel (29:22-24). He indeed sent his judgment upon an unholy people and he in truth will restore his people to a new holiness of covenantal fellowship.

Isaiah's contemporaries make little use of the name Holy One. Micah refers to the holy temple from which the LORD God will witness against his people (1:2). Amos uses the noun "holiness" in association with the Name which Israel has profaned by immoral acts (2:7); further, the LORD swears by his holiness (4:2), which means in effect by himself (cf. 6:8), to affirm that the shameless oppression of the wealthy women of Samaria shall be punished. One can observe that these two usages are similar to Isaiah's emphasis of the Holy One's judgment against sin. Although Hosea makes but one use of the name, the Holy One, it is of such unusual significance that it deserves special consideration.

Hosea

The preaching of Hosea, much like that of Isaiah, proclaimed doom and judgment upon the sins of Israel. However, in Hosea's oracles we can detect a strong tension between the pronouncements of doom and the yearnings to spare Israel from her merited judgment. This tension appears in the naming and renaming of the prophet's children. The first child's name was Jezreel, which carried the interpretation of judgment upon the house of Israel, but the name was subsequently in-

137

terpreted in terms of fertility (2:23-24 [21-22]). The second child was called Lo Ruhamah, which meant that God would not have pity on the house of Israel; but this name was changed to Ruhamah, which meant that the unpitied one would be pitied. The third child was called Lo Ammi, which was interpreted to mean that Israel was not God's people; yet later that name was changed to Ammi, meaning that Israel was God's people (1:6-2:3 [2:1]).

The struggle of soul between wrath and compassion is also expressed concerning Gomer, Hosea's unfaithful wife, who graphically represented Israel in her unfaithfulness to her LORD. Should the unfaithful wife be disowned and exposed to open shame, or should she be tenderly entreated to return to her faithful husband? (ch. 2-3). The struggle continues into the eleventh chapter where on the one hand we hear the judgment of wrath:

> The sword shall rage against their cities,
> consume the bars of their gates,
> and devour them in their fortresses.
> My people are bent on turning away from me;
> so they are appointed to the yoke,
> and none shall remove it (11:6-7).

On the other hand we hear the outcry of compassion:

> How can I give you up, O Ephraim!
> How can I hand you over, O Israel!
> How can I make you like Admah!
> How can I treat you like Zeboiim!
> My heart recoils within me,

138

> my compassion grows warm and tender.
> I will not execute my fierce anger,
> I will not again destroy Ephraim;
> for I am God and not man,
> the Holy One in your midst,
> and I will not come to destroy (11:8-9).

In this moving passage we observe that the prophet uses the name, the Holy One, in the context of being "in your midst" and with the promise "I will not come to destroy."[3] Hosea places this name in close fellowship with Israel rather than in the place of transcendence and exaltedness as does Isaiah. This name further reflects the non-consuming or saving activity of God. God will not execute his fierce anger to destroy Israel. He finds it impossible to make Israel like Admah or Zeboiim, the small cities that were caught in the destruction of Sodom and Gomorrah.

Lest one think that Hosea has ignored Isaiah's concept of transcendence, we should note that he says, "I am God and not man." The Holy One, although in the midst of men, is different from man. In this context the difference is not to be found in moral purity, as it is in Isaiah, but in the outworking of holy wrath. In Isaiah wrath brought destruction upon Israel which resulted in leaving a remnant purified. In Hosea wrath becomes heartfelt compassion which results in a love beyond human understanding that shall bring about a restored and redeemed people. The wrath of man demands the utter destruction of his foes, but the wrath of the Holy One will destroy the uncleanness in Israel, and then the Holy God will make of

Israel a new creation so that Israel shall flourish like the trees of Lebanon (14:5-7).

We have, therefore, in Hosea a double paradox built around the Holy One. The first paradox is that God comes in wrath but also in restoring power. His holy wrath comes to destroy the unholy uncleanness of Israel, but not to destroy Israel. The ultimate purpose for Israel is not her destruction but her restoration. The second paradox is that the Holy One is in the midst of man and yet is not like man. The holy wrath becomes the passion of holy love to restore the wayward people, even as Hosea restored his wayward wife. Eichrodt observes that,

> There can be no playing down the annihilating power of holiness, and the intensity of the threat of judgment in Hosea can hardly be exaggerated. Nevertheless, in the end it is *the incomprehensible creative power of love which marks out Yahweh as the wholly "other,"* the one whose nature is in complete contrast to that of the created order.[4]

The Holy One is therefore *das ganz Andere,* the completely Other, since by virtue of his holy love he brings back into holy fellowship a rebellious people, something which man would not and could not do.[5]

Deutero-Isaiah

Deutero-Isaiah, the prophet of the exile, reaches back to his predecessor in Jerusalem for the special name for God, the Holy One of Israel, and to Hosea for his messages of the LORD's re-

140

storing power and love. Hosea's unique use of the name, the Holy One, became the source and inspiration for the preaching of the great prophet in Israel's deep despair in Babylon. The first reference to the Holy One describes him as the incomparable One, "To whom then will you compare me, that I should be like him? says the Holy One" (40:25). Comparisons are made with the wisdom of men, with idols, the works of men's hands, and with nations who are like a drop in the bucket or like dust in the balance. The LORD is beyond comparison to the created world, to the people in it, and to the idols which the nations worship (40:12-24). Yet the prophet does not let that great distance between the Holy One and Israel stand unbridged, for in response to the complaint of weary Israel the prophet exclaims that the LORD the creator and the everlasting God is giving strength to those weary and faint (40:27-31). Here the prophet has set the theme for his messages: The Holy One shall come to bring restoration and redemption to his people.

Two names which are significantly used as appositives to the Holy One are the Creator, *bôre'*, and the Redeemer, *go'el*. Although other titles such as Savior, King, Maker, and Husband appear, yet the prophet seems especially attracted to Creator and Redeemer in his message of comfort to Israel. To grasp the meaning of these two names will further enrich our understanding of the Holy One.

The LORD, the Holy One, is the Creator of Israel. Since he is the one who formed Israel, who

141

created Jacob, he will not abandon his creation, for they are his (43:1). He will gather his children whom he has created for his glory from the east and the west, and he will command the north and the south to bring forth his sons and daughters whom he has formed and made for his glory (43:5-7). The Holy One of Israel will break the strength of Babylon and he will bring lamentation upon the Chaldeans, for the Creator of Israel, her King, is about to lead his people out of their captivity (43:14-15).

The prophet declares that the LORD has aroused Cyrus to become his anointed to deliver Israel out of exile (45:1). The prophet anticipates that some in Israel will object against the use of a pagan prince to perform God's purposes. He therefore proclaims this oracle against this supposed objection:

> Woe to him who strives with his Maker,
> an earthen vessel with the potter!
> Does the clay say to him who fashions it,
> "What are you making?"
> or "Your work has no handles?"
> Woe to him who says to a father,
> "What are you begetting?"
> or to a woman, "With what are you in travail?"
> (45:9-10).

As Creator the Holy One of Israel is sovereign, for he not only brings Israel into being, but also sets up Cyrus as a creation of his hands so that this Cyrus may open the way and build the city in which the returned exiles may live. The LORD as Creator is, on the one hand, the Maker of Israel,

142

his covenant people, and on the other hand brings into being the Persian king who shall further God's purpose for Israel (45:11-13).

The creation of Cyrus, as described in the above-mentioned passage, subordinates the factor of creation to the purpose of redemption in history. It is not enough to say that Cyrus was formed by God, for he was brought forth to take his place on the stage of history. We should note further that the LORD's acts in the creation of people and nature are of secondary importance since these intend to advance his purpose of salvation for Israel. His marvels of creation promote his designs as Redeemer. We can note that subordinate clauses such as "[he] who creates the heavens" and "[he] who created you, O Jacob, he who formed you, O Israel" (42:5; 43:1) are designed to heighten the description of the redemption which is to take place.[6] The Holy One, who is indeed the Creator of the ends of the earth, is the One who brings new strength to weary Israel (40:25-29). In fact, the prophet actually presents creation as a continuing event in history. The salvation which is to come is regarded as the new creation not known before:

> From this time I make you hear new things,
> hidden things which you have not known.
> They are created now, not long ago;
> before today you have never heard of them (48:6-7).

To be sure, the LORD is the one who brought out the starry host by number (40:26) and who laid the foundations of the earth and spread out the heavens (48:13), but his primary role as

Creator has to do with his acts of redemption in history.[7]

Other names associated with the Holy One are Redeemer and Savior, which supplement and elaborate his work as Creator. The name Redeemer embodies the feelings which the Israelite had for the honor and welfare of his family. Should a member of a family be reduced to such poverty that he would sell himself into slavery, then his brother or relative would be obliged to pay his debt and redeem him out of slavery so that the name of the family would not be dishonored. The redeemer, called *go'el*, defended the family against disgrace, and he saw to it that the family name should not become extinct. According to this prophet of the exile, the LORD will now act to defend the honor of his holy name which has been profaned by Israel's captors, as Ezekiel declared, "when they came to the nations, wherever they came, they profaned my holy name, in that men said of them, 'These are the people of the LORD, and yet they had to go out of his land'" (Ezek. 36:20). Furthermore our prophet declares that Israel has endured more than enough affliction (Isa. 40:2); that Babylon in her pride has made the yoke of captivity exceedingly heavy (47:6-7); and that Israel, God's people, has been despised and abhorred by the nations and has become a slave to haughty rulers (49:7). The Holy One of Israel shall come to redeem her from that disgrace and affliction (49:26).

As the Redeemer of Israel the LORD takes into account her weak and humble condition described as a worm under the heel of Babylon; yet Israel shall become strong and her captors shall become chaff blown from the threshing floor (41:14-16). Much is made of the downfall of Babylon as the LORD comes to redeem his people from exile (43:14; 47:1-5). Even though Israel is weak and poor, yet she is very precious to the LORD her Redeemer and he pays as ransom the mighty and wealthy nations of Egypt and Ethiopia (43:3-4); thus the LORD does not choose the rich and mighty to become his people (cf. Deut. 7:7-8). We can sense that the LORD has undying love for Israel, his people in distress, and this is described in terms of a husband bringing back to himself his wife who had been forsaken for awhile:

> For the LORD has called you
> like a wife forsaken and grieved in spirit,
> like a wife of youth when she is cast off,
> says your God.
> For a brief moment I forsook you,
> but with great compassion I will gather you.
> In overflowing wrath for a moment I hid my face
> from you,
> but with everlasting love I will have compassion
> on you,
> says the LORD, your Redeemer (54:6-8).

We are especially reminded here of Hosea's restoration of Gomer as the symbol of God's outgoing love for Israel. And further we can clearly perceive that the Holy One, whose burning wrath in Hosea's famous oracle gave way to tender compassion to restore and save Israel, here speaks through this prophet in terms of love beyond human understanding which allows wrath to burn for a moment,

145

but which finally turns to great compassion. In both prophets the wonder of redeeming love is manifested in the Holy One of Israel.

Another significant association with Hosea in Deutero-Isaiah is that the Holy One lives in the midst of his people. "I am God and not man, the Holy One in your midst" (Hos. 11:9). So also this prophet sees the Holy One in close fellowship with the stricken and humble people in exile:

> For thus says the high and lofty One
> who inhabits eternity, whose name is Holy:
> "I dwell in the high and holy place,
> and also with him who is of a contrite and humble
>   spirit,
> to revive the spirit of the humble,
> and to revive the heart of the contrite. . ." (57:15).

In this moving utterance he combines the transcendence of the Holy One as seen by Isaiah in Jerusalem and the nearness of the Holy One as declared by Hosea. This prophet, therefore, standing in the momentous time of Israel's redemptive experience, sees the full-orbed manifestation of the Holy One of Israel, who in overflowing compassion subdues wrath to redeem his people.

The above survey on holiness as ascribed to God offers an important balance to the common conception of God, the Holy One, as the Complete Other. To be sure, we ought not forget the elements of unapproachability and purity which Isaiah stressed, since the LORD is God and there is none else. But to restrict the meaning of holiness to the complete otherness of God and to his absolute separation from man, especially from sinful man, is to ignore the witness of Hosea who saw the Holy One with infinite compassion within Israel to make salvation and restoration his final purpose for Israel. Deutero-Isaiah elaborated this theme as he proclaimed the coming of the Holy One to be the Redeemer and Creator of his helpless and forlorn people in exile. Is the Holy One high and lifted up? Yes, but more, for the Holy One is in the midst of his people, he dwells in the heart of the contrite. He will be glorified in his redeemed people (41:16), and he will glorify Israel, his witness to the nations (43:10-12; 55:4f.).

> Since then Jahweh as the Holy One (*Qadosh*) is God and not man, since he stands over against the natural law of creation, since his thought and ways are not the ways of man (55:8-9), therefore his holiness corresponds to a new creation (*kaine ktisis*) in which he is all in all, since the former things (*ta archaia*) have passed away, and everything has become new.[8]

How appropriate is the praise of the prophet:

> Sing, O heavens, for the LORD has done it;
> shout, O depths of the earth;
> break forth into singing, O mountains,
> O forest, and every tree in it!
> For the LORD has redeemed Jacob,
> and will be glorified in Israel (44:23).

The Holy Spirit in the New Testament

In this part of our study we shall attempt to relate some concepts that are inherent in the name of the Holy One of Israel to the Holy Spirit of the

147

New Testament. Stated more precisely, our purpose shall be to concentrate on the points of emphasis made by the great prophet of the exile to determine whether these emphases are taken up in the person and work of the Holy Spirit.

Since in the New Testament we deal with God as revealed in three persons, we shall first observe how seldom "holy" is attached to God, the Father. The following survey lists the instances in which this occurs. In his upper-room prayer, in which he petitions God to keep his disciples in the fellowship of unity, Jesus addresses God as Holy Father (Jn. 17:11). In the prayer which Jesus taught his disciples the name of God is to be made or kept holy (Mt. 6:9; Lk. 11:2). In Mary's hymn of praise, apparently taken from Psalm 111:9, she declares that God's name is holy as she celebrates his great mercy and strength (Lk. 1:49). In I Peter 1:15-16 the apostle appeals to Leviticus 19:2 and declares that since God is holy, Christians are also to be holy. This reference combines holiness with purity of life, for the holy ones, *hagioi,* must be the pure ones, *hagnoi.* The Trisagion of praise is offered to the Lord God Almighty (Rev. 4:8); "holy" and "true" are titles ascribed to the sovereign Lord (6:10) and are also descriptive of the Son (3:7). Although holiness is seldom attributed to God, the Father, in the New Testament, we ought not therefore conclude that concepts of divine transcendence, wrath, and purity are unknown, for much of the Old Testament holiness is latent, if not patent, in the New Testament teachings about the Father.

148

Our next concern is to learn to what extent holiness is related to Jesus Christ. In the annunciation of the angel Gabriel to the virgin Mary, it is declared that the child to be born shall be called holy, the Son of God (Lk. 1:35). The witness of the demons, as Jesus begins his ministry of teaching and healing, is: "What have you to do with us, Jesus of Nazareth? Have you come to destroy us? I know who you are, the Holy One of God" (Mk. 1:24; Lk. 4:34). The demons see here the downfall of their kingdom as Jesus begins to establish the kingdom of God which is now at hand (Mk. 1:15). As spokesman for the twelve, Peter makes the confession of faith to declare that Jesus is the Holy One of God (Jn. 6:69). In the same gospel Jesus asserts that he has been made holy by the Father and sent into the world, and therefore he may rightly claim to be the Son of God (10:36). In the early parts of Acts references are made to Jesus as the Holy Servant, and these are clear allusions to the Servant of the Lord prophecies of Isaiah (Acts 3:14; 4:27,30). In the first epistle of John the anointing by the Holy One is undoubtedly a play on the name Christ, the Anointed, who is the One to anoint the believers (2:20). Finally, as noted above, Christ is given the title of Holy One by John on the island of Patmos (Rev. 3:7). Here we may note, as we did ·in the previous paragraph, that holiness is not frequently attributed to Jesus Christ, yet the few references indicate his special relationship with God in establishing the kingdom of God among man.

The above survey reveals that the word "holy"

149

is not commonly associated with the Father or the Son. This infrequency becomes even more pronounced when we note how frequently it is associated with the Spirit. A concordance tabulation discloses that in the 111 instances that Spirit is used as referring to God, the adjective "holy" is attached eighty-nine times.[9] The New Testament usage apparently identified "holy" with the Spirit so fully that the adjective seemed inappropriate with either the Father or the Son.

Holy Spirit was a name in common use among the Jews who used it and other names to avoid speaking the name Jahweh. It hardly seems likely, however, that Christians took over the name from the Jews, for that would blur the significance of Pentecost by giving a Jewish name for God to the promised Paraclete. It seems more reasonable to assume that the Christian church not only regarded the Holy Spirit's coming as a fulfillment of the Old Testament promise, but also declared that the redemptive manifestations of the Holy One of Israel were now to be realized and fulfilled in the Holy Spirit.

We cannot hope to identify all the concepts about God given in the Old Testament with those of the New Testament, and such is not our purpose here. Further, we cannot cover all that pertains to the doctrine of the Holy Spirit in this brief discussion. Rather, our objective is definitive; we wish to note as clearly as possible that what we have discovered to be the understanding of God's holiness in the Old Testament is basic to our understanding of the Holy Spirit in the New Testament. We shall delineate three concepts that come into clear focus: fellowship, creation, and redemption. These three occupy a significant place in our comprehension of the Holy One of Israel, especially in the preaching of Deutero-Isaiah.

1. Fellowship. Even though holiness expresses the complete otherness of God and his unapproachability, yet it describes God in fellowship with Israel and dwelling in the spirit of the humble and contrite. So also in the writings of the apostle Paul we are told that believers are the temple of the Holy Spirit and that God dwells in this temple (I Cor. 3:16-17; 6:19; Eph. 2:21-22). As the Holy Spirit once dwelt in Israel in Mosaic times (cf. Is. 63:10-11), so now the Holy Spirit lives in the redeemed community because he is given to the church for purity of life (I Thess. 4:7-8). The Apostle enjoins Timothy to follow the pattern of sound words and to guard the truth by the power of the indwelling Holy Spirit (II Tim. 1:13-14). Paul uses the Holy Spirit only once in his benediction and that is to express the fellowship of the Holy Spirit (II Cor. 13:14), which may be interpreted to mean a fellowship with the Spirit, or a fellowship which the Spirit creates within the body of believers. In each case the fellowship which the church enjoys proceeds from the Holy Spirit. Because of the indwelling Holy Spirit believers are brought into one body and in that one body they are to receive the diversity of gifts from the Spirit (I Cor. 12:4-13).

2. Creation. The Spirit is the mighty Creator who can repeat the miracle of the resurrection of

151

Christ in the believer. The man who lives according to the dictates of the flesh is dead, and man's plight is all the more desperate in that his attempts to escape this death are futile. Paul asserts, however, that the same Spirit that raised Jesus from the dead (cf. Rom. 1:4) can also dwell within the believer and give life to his mortal body (Rom. 8:11). Through the Spirit a renewal and strengthening take place within the inner man. The man in Christ becomes a new creation, for the old things have passed away (II Cor. 5:17). This mortal, in which we now find ourselves, yearns to be swallowed up by life, which will indeed take place, for God has given us the Spirit as a guarantee for the new creation (II Cor. 5:4-5).

Baptism symbolizes a new relationship of the believer united to Christ in his death so that in that union with Christ the believer may be raised to walk in newness of life (Rom. 5:3-5; Col. 2:12; 3:1-2). The Spirit's power is present in baptism, for it is through one Spirit that all are baptized into one body, and all are made to drink of one Spirit (I Cor. 12:13). The new creation, both the believer himself and fellowship of believers, is nothing less than the Holy Spirit's bringing to manifestation again and again that same power which raised Jesus from the dead.

Here one notes a remarkable counterpart to God's raising Israel out of the death of exile into which she went because of her transgression of the holy covenant and out of which she was unable to deliver herself. The prophet of the exile declared that the Holy One was the Creator and Maker of a

152

restored people in which the former things were done away with and the day of Israel's new life was to begin. In the New Testament the resurrection of Christ through the power of the Holy Spirit makes a new creation possible. This is the possibility which the church, the new Israel, experiences as each believer is raised by the Spirit from his death in sin to walk in newness of life. This indeed becomes a new creation; "the old has passed away, behold, the new has come" (II Cor. 5:17).

3. Redemption. As Redeemer of Israel the Holy One continues his work through the Holy Spirit in the New Testament. Redemption is greatly needed since, according to Paul, both Jews and Gentiles are held in bondage. For the Jew this is a bondage under the law; and for the Gentile it is a bondage to the powers of the world, or to those beings that are no gods. All are redeemed from this bondage as God sends forth "the Spirit of his Son into our hearts, crying 'Abba! Father!'" (Gal. 4:6). Slaves in bondage are now released from fear to enjoy the status of children of God through the witness of the Spirit (Rom. 8:14-16). A radical transformation takes place in the believer by means of the "washing of regeneration and renewal in the Holy Spirit" (Tit. 3:5), for this renewal delivers those who are now "heirs in hope of eternal life" (ver. 7) from their former condition as "slaves to various passions and pleasures, passing our days in malice and envy, hated by men and hating one another" (ver. 3). The redemptive power of the Spirit continues in that those who walk by the Spirit will not again submit to the

bondage of the flesh or to that of the law (Gal. 5:16-18). Indeed, the redemption once begun in the believer by the Spirit reaches an ecstatic consummation. The believer is assured the hope of righteousness (Gal. 5:5), the future resurrection (II Cor. 4:13-14), the redemption of the body (Rom. 8:23), and the reaping of eternal life (Gal. 6:8). These eschatological hopes are all the assurance of the believer who awaits the consummation of his redemption through the Holy Spirit.

Our study discloses that the Old Testament data about the holiness of God carry over in large measure into the work of the Holy Spirit of the New Testament. As in the Old Testament, so also in the New, holiness has to do with redemption and salvation. In each case God takes the initiative to redeem man from his hopeless death, and in each case man is brought into a new life of freedom which reaches forward into a consummation far beyond human understanding. The Holy One of Israel makes his redeemed people his witnesses and they declare that he is the LORD and that besides him there is no savior (Is. 43:10-11). This has its remarkable counterpart in Paul's famous declaration, "no one can say 'Jesus is Lord!' except by the Holy Spirit" (I Cor. 12:3; cf. Rom. 8:16). What the Holy One did for Israel prefigures what the Holy Spirit has done and is doing for all people who are in Christ.

All this highlights a fundamental understanding about the holiness of God, in that holiness is not a static formal definition about the being of God, but rather God in vital dynamic relationship with man to deliver him from his desperate plight and to set him in a new life which offers him the fellowship and benefits of the children of God.

NOTES

1. W. Eichrodt, *Theology of the Old Testament*, Vol. I (Philadelphia: The Westminster Press, 1961), pp. 270-71; for a discussion on etymology see N. H. Snaith, *The Distinctive Ideas of the Old Testament* (Philadelphia: The Westminster Press, 1946), pp. 24-38.

2. Verbs such as "hallow," "sanctify," and "consecrate" are translations of the causative stems of the Hebrew verb *QDSH*, which literally would be "cause to be holy, make holy."

3. Since the Hebrew text *be'îr*, "in a city," yields little sense, it seems proper to accept the emendation *leba'er*, "to destroy."

4. Eichrodt, *op. cit.*, p. 281.

5. O. Procksch makes this discerning comment:

> In the older Hebrew concept the divine stands in mortal opposition to the human and especially the sinful. This opposition remains in Hosea's view of God, but it is absorbed into the opposition of holy love to unholy nature. What God in virtue of His holiness may do to love unholy nature, no man may do, and therefore the antithesis between God and man consists in the very love which overcomes it.

Theological Dictionary of the New Testament, Vol. I (Grand Rapids: Wm. B. Eerdmans Publishing Co., 1964), p. 93.

6. Cf. G. von Rad, *Old Testament Theology*, Vol. I (New York: Harper & Brothers, 1962), pp. 137-39.

7. Th. C. Vriezen in the discussion of the theology of creation points up both creation as secondary to history and creation as a continuing process by which this world is to be transformed into the kingdom of God; *An Outline of Old Testament Theology* (Boston: Charles T. Branford Company, 1958), pp. 346ff., 361ff.

8. Procksch, *op. cit.*, p. 94.

9. J. B. Smith, *Greek-English Concordance to the New Testament* (Scottdale, Pennsylvania: Herald Press, 1955), p. 296.

CHAPTER VI

GRACE AND TRUTH: IN THE OLD TESTAMENT AND IN THE GOSPEL OF JOHN

THE PROLOGUE OF THE GOSPEL OF JOHN GIVES this significant description of the Word that became flesh: "And the Word became flesh and dwelt among us, full of grace and truth" (Jn. 1:14). The expression "full of grace and truth" is Old Testament language which occurs frequently in various forms when a prophet or psalmist is speaking about God. It is not surprising that the evangelist takes this term from the Old Testament, for, in the prologue, not to mention the rest of the Gospel, there are several allusions to the Old Testament, including reference to the beginning and creation, reference to Moses and the law, and the allusion to seeing God, or rather to the fact that no one has seen God at any time. When John therefore declares that the incarnate Word is "full of grace and truth" he is telling his readers to look for the meaning of this expression in the Old Testament where it is descriptive of God. Notice, for example, the following Old Testament quotation which embodies other descriptive words about God: "The LORD passed before him [Moses], and proclaimed, 'The LORD, the LORD, a God merciful

157

and gracious, slow to anger, and abounding in steadfast love and faithfulness' " (Ex 34:6). In John's Gospel "abounding in steadfast love and faithfulness" becomes "full of grace and truth."[1]

A proper interpretation of the Johannine "grace and truth" must reckon with the Old Testament meaning of these words. The purpose of this chapter is to establish the Old Testament usage and then to determine whether the evangelist was relying on the Old Testament background when he declared that the incarnate Word was "full of grace and truth," or whether he was relying on the meaning of these words in current Greek literature.

Grace

Our study begins with grace, the first quality of God in the pair mentioned in the prologue formulation, "full of grace and truth." Its counterpart in the Old Testament is the Hebrew word *ḥesedh,* which is variously given by the King James Version as "mercy," "goodness," and "lovingkindness," and which is usually translated "steadfast love" in the Revised Standard Version. Since no one English word will suffice to convey its meaning, we shall use the Hebrew word *ḥesed* throughout this chapter.

In his doctoral dissertation, *Das Wort Ḥesed im alttestamentliche Sprachgebrauch,* Nelson Glueck has made a significant contribution to the understanding of this word in the Hebrew Bible.[2] His work has left its effect upon subsequent biblical

158

scholarship as can be seen in the recent lexicon of Koehler-Baumgartner which reflects the results of Glueck's research.

Professor Glueck has rightly discerned that there is a profane as well as a religious use for *hesed*. In the so-called secular or profane usage this word refers to the relationship among men. Let us note a few such references.

Shortly before his death Jacob summoned his son Joseph and said, "If now I have found favor in your sight, put your hand under my thigh, and do for me *hesed* and faithfulness. Do not bury me in Egypt" (Gen. 47:29). In the father-son relationship Jacob asked his son Joseph to show loyalty and fidelity to his father in the matter of burying him with the fathers in Canaan. Joseph solemnly confirmed this request with an oath. In the setting of a husband-wife relationship Abraham required Sarah to perform *hesed*, namely, that she would say that she was Abraham's sister. They agreed upon this lie in order to protect Abraham from the lustful avarice of those who might want to make Sarah a widow. Abraham therefore appealed to Sarah to perform *hesed*, that is loyalty, to her husband, by saying that she was his sister (20:13). In another scene of family relationship Abraham's servant appeals to Bethuel, the father, and Laban, the brother, to demonstrate their *hesed* and truth toward Abraham, the servant's lord. He appeals that they may show loyalty to and respect for the family bond (24:49). To do *hesed* is to demonstrate faithfulness and loyalty toward the members within the family bond.

159

In the well-known story of Ruth, who had forsaken her family tie and friends in Moab to unite herself with the family and faith of her deceased husband, which she was apparently not under obligation to do, it is interesting to note that Boaz makes this significant appraisal of Ruth's conduct: "Blessed are you of the LORD, my daughter, for you have performed a more beautiful *ḥesed* now than at the first in that you did not go after young men either poor or rich" (Ruth 3:10). Boaz is noting that Ruth had done two *ḥeseds,* the first in demonstrating her loyalty to her husband's family by following Naomi back to Israel, and the second in seeking marriage with the old Boaz, a relative of her deceased husband, in order to raise up seed for her deceased husband. This, says Boaz, was an even greater *ḥesed* than the first act of family loyalty. In a previous incident Boaz had also shown an act of *ḥesed* in ordering his men to allow Ruth to glean where there were many sheaves. In this he showed a devotion and loyalty to his family (2:20).

In less intimate relationships *ḥesed* appears as evidence of profound regard for the association or fellowship established between two or more people. Such relationship appears in a host-guest setting in which both the host and the guest perform *ḥesed* toward each other, as in the case of Lot and his heavenly guests at Sodom (Gen. 19:19), or in the case of Rahab and the spies (Josh. 2:12,14). The loyalty between David and Jonathan is another instance of *ḥesed* (I Sam. 20:8,14,15). Later, in honoring the covenant established with the deceased Jonathan, David sought opportunity to show *hesed* to the house of Saul (II Sam. 9:1,3,7).

Other examples of *hesed* in man-to-man relationships can be added,[3] but these will suffice to demonstrate that in the performance of *hesed* one expects to find loyalty, mutual reciprocity, genuine faithfulness or brotherly love, and affection. *Hesed* is not an outburst of unlooked-for mercy, nor an arbitrary demonstration of favor. Within a covenant or fellowship or family circle members of the fellowship demonstrate *hesed* by fidelity and loyalty to each other. Perhaps it should be noted that members either willingly entered these relationships, or naturally grew into the fellowship as was the case within a family. Each member therefore willingly practiced this *hesed* toward those in the fellowship and expected it from others. As long as the relationship was vital, so long would *hesed* continue.

Truth

The second word for our study is "truth," which we shall designate by its Hebrew word *'emeth,* also *'emûnah.* Our English translation "truth" has unfortunately rendered some misunderstanding of the Hebrew *emeth,* even as mercy or lovingkindness creates some misunderstanding of *hesed.*

The noun *'emeth* is derived from the verb *'aman,* which means being "steady, firm, and dependable." The verb appears largely in the causative stem, which suggests the idea of having

161

confidence and firmness, and might be expressed in our language as exercising faith and trust. In an interesting play on the verbal root Isaiah tells king Ahaz, "If you will not exercise trust [active voice], you will not become established [passive voice]" (Is. 7:9). This manipulation of the verbal root clearly suggests that the root embraced concepts of faith, confidence, and stability. The nounal forms from this root would naturally reflect similar concepts such as faithfulness and dependability. Thus, *emeth* in its use with *shalom,* commonly translated peace or welfare, would signify a condition of permanent security (Is. 39:8; Jer. 33:6).

Persons who have *emeth,* such as the judges Moses is advised to appoint, are dependable (Ex. 18:21). So also Hananiah is appointed to be the governor of the castle because of his noteworthy dependability (Neh. 7:2). The people of Israel are urged to serve the LORD in *emeth,* that is, faithfulness (Josh. 24:14; I Sam. 12:24). The reference from Samuel adds that to serve the LORD faithfully involves the entire heart (cf. I Kings 2:4).

Emeth is frequently combined with *ḥesed,* a combination which describes a relationship in which loyal faithfulness can be expected. In the incident concerning Eliezer, Bethuel, and Laban, Eliezer asks them to do both *ḥesed* and *emeth* toward Abraham by granting the request that Rebekah may become the wife of Isaac (Gen. 24:49); thus also Jacob asks Joseph to perform both *ḥesed* and *emeth* in taking the oath to bury him in Canaan (47:29). The spies, in response to Rahab's sheltering them, solemnly promise that

162

they will show her *hesed* and *emeth* when Israel takes possession of the land (Josh. 2:14). The prophet Hosea declares that "There is no *emeth* and no *hesed* and no knowledge of God in the land" (4:1). In the next verse this is explained to mean that there is swearing, lying, killing, stealing, and adultery, all evidences of lack of faithfulness and dependability. The wise man in Proverbs says, "*Hesed* and *emeth* preserve the king, and his throne is upheld by *hesed*" (20:28).

From the above we can observe that *emeth* carries meanings which also appear in *hesed*, so that when they are combined as a hendiadys the second term intends to confirm and enrich the first. Each of the two concerns relationships rather than concepts and ideas. As we shall learn presently, they come to apply largely to the covenant in which God deals with Israel according to *hesed* and *emeth*.

We need to examine another word in order to sharpen our understanding of the two already discussed. This third word is *hen*, which very closely approximates the English word "grace" as it is commonly understood in theological usage. In fact, in its nounal, adjectival, and verbal forms, *hen* is translated as grace, gracious, and to be gracious. *Hen* or *hanan*, its verbal root, indicates a favor which a superior offers an inferior. The superior is under no obligation to grant the favor, yet out of the goodness of his heart may choose to give the one of lower rank a consideration which could not be claimed or demanded.

Professor Lofthouse, in his article "*Hen* and

163

Hesed in the Old Testament,"[4] illustrates this type of consideration in cases such as the story of Shechem, who asked to find *hen* in the eyes of Jacob and the brothers of Dinah whom he wished to marry (Gen. 34:11), or Joseph who found *hen* in the eyes of Potiphar (39:4), or the Egyptians who asked to find *hen* in the sight of Joseph (47:25). Even Jacob the father appealed to the *hen* of his son Joseph when he asked that Joseph bury him in the land of Canaan (47:29). Here it appears that Jacob recognized his son's superior status and therefore sought *hen* from him but—let it be carefully noted—he also placed Joseph within the bond of the family when he asked Joseph to perform *hesed* and *emeth,* which, as we noted above, was the faithful loyalty that should mark the relationships within the Hebrew family. In this touching scene involving Jacob and Joseph we detect the distinction between *hen* and *hesed*: *hen* is a gracious, unmerited favor which a superior bestows on an inferior; *hesed* is also an act of goodness, but one that can be expected since it takes place within the context of a covenant of intimate fellowship. If the covenant is between unequals or between equals, *hesed* can be performed by either party, for through *hesed* the covenant is maintained and the relationship within the fellowship manifests vitality.

Our brief survey of these words in the profane life of Israel will serve as background to study them as they are used about the LORD, the God of Israel, for it seems reasonable that Israel would use the vocabulary of the common life to describe

164

its relationship to God. It is in words such as *hesed*
that we arrive at an understanding of such relationships. Here of necessity we struggle with words
and phrases of another language in order to
express through them the concepts that words like
hesed and *emeth* carried for the ancient Hebrew.

Translations

The difficulties of translating the Bible accurately have beset translators ancient and modern. A
pen from the past, that of the grandson who bears
the same name as his grandfather, Jesus Sirach,
writes in the introduction to the apocryphal book
Ecclesiasticus that

> what was originally expressed in Hebrew does not
> have exactly the same sense when translated into
> another language. Not only this work, but even
> the law itself, the prophecies, and the rest of the
> books differ not a little as originally expressed.

Every Bible student will give hearty assent to this
observation. To this we would add that words or
phrases of the Old Testament have been rendered
as certain specific expressions in ancient translations, and in some instances this has confined these
words to specific concepts from which they may be
rescued with laborious difficulty. We have attempted such a rescue in the case of *hesed* and
emeth.

Let us trace the course of translation through
which *hesed* ran. The first translation of the Old
Testament Hebrew was a Greek version known as
the Septuagint (LXX). This version rendered

hesed as *eleos,* which meant pity, and the Latin Vulgate followed with *misericordia,* which also has the sense of pity. The early church fathers followed this line of thought and used words that meant pity, compassion, or tenderness. In ancient dictionaries such as that of Brian Walton (1657) and another by John Taylor (1754) both of which are built on the works of the Buxtorfs, who flourished in the late sixteenth and first half of the seventeenth centuries, *hesed* is interpreted as goodness, kindness, beneficence, pity. The early English translations usually have what we observe in the King James Version, mercy, lovingkindness, and goodness. The word *hesed* thus ran in this course of thought until recent times when, thanks to the work of Nelson Glueck noted above, it became clear that it was used by the ancient Hebrews to describe a relationship of loyalty and mutual responsibility to members within the covenant or within any other established fellowship.

Hesed caused the Revised Standard Version committee so much difficulty, we are told, that they could not find one English word that would satisfactorily carry its meaning. Consequently, they resorted to two words, steadfast love. Perhaps, in the course of time, usage will combine the two into one word, "steadfastlove," much like "lovingkindness."[5]

Emeth, commonly translated truth, was so rendered by the LXX. Procksch informs us that of the ninety-two instances of *emeth* the LXX translated it *alêtheia,* truth, eighty-six times, and *pistis,* faith, only six times.[6] *Emunah,* the other nounal form,

166

was rendered *alêtheia* twenty-one times and *pistis* nineteen times. The Vulgate followed the LXX in translating these words as "truth." So it was that "truth" became the translation for the English versions until the beginning of our century. Biblical scholarship has now determined that *emeth* and *emunah* were words that described relationships of faithfulness and steadfastness and were not words for abstractions of thought such as the Greek *alêtheia* suggested. Consequently today our lexicons offer "faithfulness," "steadfastness," and even "faith," which the LXX also used in some instances.

The *Ḥesed* and *Emeth* of the LORD

In our study to this point we have observed that *ḥesed* and *emeth* as used in the common life of Israel described loyalty and faithfulness in daily relationships, many of which involved covenant. It was also in the covenantal relationship that the LORD manifested his *ḥesed* and *emeth* to Israel. In the chapter on the covenant we learned that two kinds of covenants were known among Israel's neighbors, the covenant of a superior with an inferior, and the covenant between equals. It is in the former type that the LORD related himself to Israel.

The question of God's motivation in establishing the covenant with Israel can only be answered in terms of a bestowal of unmerited favor.

It was not because you were more in number than any other people that the LORD set his love upon

167

> you and chose you, for you were the fewest of all peoples; but it is because the LORD loves you, and is keeping the oath which he swore to your fathers, that the LORD has brought you out with a mighty hand, and redeemed you from the house of bondage, from the hand of Pharaoh king of Egypt (Deut. 7:7-8).

This, in the language of Paul, would be called *charis*, grace. Although *hen*, favor, is not used in the making of covenants, it would seem to be the word especially suited to describe the condescending grace of God for Israel.

The wonder of God's favor in the covenant is that he keeps the covenant and his *hesed* with those within the covenant, for "the LORD your God is God, the faithful [verbal root of *emeth*] God who keeps covenant and *hesed* with those who love him and keep his commandments" (Deut. 7:9). In the great prayer of dedication of the temple king Solomon addresses God as one who keeps covenant and demonstrates *hesed* (I Kings 8:23; II Chron. 6:14; cf. also Neh. 1:5; 9:32).

Israel was under obligation to keep the covenant by obeying the commandments, something which she persistently failed to do. Although the LORD in his wrath sent affliction and punishment upon his people, yet he constantly remembered his covenant and displayed anew his *hesed* to restore them. In the acts of restoration *hesed* appears to take on the sense of unmerited favor which is repeatedly manifested toward wayward Israel. Perhaps we should understand unmerited favor to be a constant overtone in *hesed*, enriching

168

the main concept of the LORD's faithfulness to his covenant.

This same concept of faithfulness is found in the covenant made with David where the prophet Nathan declares,

> I will be his father, and he shall be my son. When he commits iniquity, I will chasten him with the rod of men, with the stripes of the sons of men; but I will not take my *hesed* from him, as I took it away from Saul (II Sam. 7:14-15).

Here was established a father-son relationship which would express itself in *hesed,* God's faithful concern for David, and the faithfulness of David and his seed toward God. If David did not manifest *hesed* he would be chastened with the rod of men. The establishing of this covenant with David is celebrated in Psalm 89, in which three terms interplay on the one theme: *berith,* covenant, *emunah,* faithfulness, and *hesed,* steadfastness, all of which comprise the theme of God's faithfulness to David.

> I will sing of thy *hesed,* O LORD, for ever;
> with my mouth I will proclaim thy *emunah* to all generations.
> For thy *hesed* was established for ever,
> thy *emunah* is firm as the heavens.
> Thou hast said, "I have made a *berith* with my chosen one,
> I have sworn to David my servant:
> 'I will establish your descendants for ever,
> and build your throne for all generations' " (89:2-5 [1-4]).

> "I will not remove from him my *hesed,*
> or be false to my *emunah.*

169

> I will not violate my *berith*,
> or alter the word that went forth from my lips"
> (89:34-35 [33-34]).[7]

These three words also appear in the promise made by the prophet in Isaiah 55:3, "I will make with you an everlasting covenant, the dependable *ḥesed* of David." Glueck interprets "the faithful *ḥesed* of David" as the normative faithful relationship which God exercises through the covenant.[8]

Ḥesed as the LORD's covenantal loyalty to Israel may be observed in some of the prophets. In Hosea God contemplates bringing Israel back into the God-people relationship. Israel has become a wayward wife like Gomer, the wife of Hosea, but after God has subjected Israel to severe punishment, he will then allure her into the desert as in the days when Israel was first beloved of God, when God loved Israel and called his people out of Egypt (11:1). There Israel will answer God as at the time she came out of Egypt, and God will then betroth her to himself for ever. "I will betroth you to me in *emunah*" (2:21 [19]). In this setting the LORD will restore Israel in three realms of experience: in righteousness and justice, which reflects the moral or ethical life, in *ḥesed* and *emunah*, which reflect God's reliability, and in mercy, which reflects God's love and tenderness in forgiving wayward Israel.

The prophet of the exile speaks about the LORD, the Redeemer of Israel, who will have compassion with eternal *ḥesed* on Israel, and his *ḥesed* shall not depart from Israel nor shall the covenant of his peace be removed (Is. 54:8-10). *Ḥesed* is here paralleled with covenant and mercy.

170

God's covenant includes both love and loyalty for his people.

In the Psalms the formal declaration about the LORD being "full of *hesed* and *emeth*" (Ex. 34:6) takes on a liturgical form such as, "For his *hesed* endures for ever" (Ps. 136; cf. also 106:1; 107:1). The psalmist recalls the many deliverances experienced by Israel for which the people are to give thanks to the LORD, "for his *hesed*, for his wonderful works to the sons of men" (107:8,15,21, 31). Consequently, in some psalms *hesed* becomes a synonym for salvation or deliverance in which Israel can trust (6:5 [4]; 31:17 [16]; 44:27 [26]; 109:21).

Although *emeth* does not become a liturgical formula in the Psalms, it does appear in combinations with *hesed* concerning God, as noted above (25:10; 40:11-12 [10-11]; 86:15). In these cases *emeth* describes God's faithfulness and dependability. These qualities are also ascribed to the law or commandments in which the godly may trust (19:10 [9]; 119:30, 43, 86, 142, 151, 160). Whereas both *hesed* and *emeth* relate to the concept of the reliability of both the LORD and his law, *hesed* may apparently also suggest the concept of deliverance and salvation.

Sin and Forgiveness

In our chapter on the covenant we raised the problem of Israel's forsaking or breaking the covenant. Although we observed that the LORD in no case renounced the covenant, yet it was necessary that Israel's sin should be forgiven for her to remain in the covenant. For our present purpose we wish to determine whether forgiveness is part of the LORD's *ḥesed* for Israel. Or does forgiveness result from his unmerited favor toward his wayward people?

Professor Glueck has offered a discerning insight as an answer to the above.[9] He concludes from his exegesis of Numbers 14:18-19 that God forgives because of his grace, and because of his compassion. This is an act of unqualified grace. And because Israel's sin is forgiven, God's faithful loyalty to Israel comes to full manifestation. Glueck recalls that God's choice of Israel was an act of pure grace. The covenant with Israel rests upon unmerited favor, that is, upon *ḥen*. Within that covenant, as we noted before, God performed his *ḥesed* and *emeth,* steadfastness and faithfulness. So it is in the matter of the forgiveness of sin which breaks the covenant; the breach is healed because God is gracious and compassionate. When forgiveness and consequent restoration have taken place, then we read in the longer statement of the formula in Exodus 34:6 that the LORD abounds in *ḥesed* and *emeth* in that he is keeping *ḥesed* for thousands, even as the second commandment (Ex. 20:6) states that God performs his *ḥesed* to thousands who love him and keep his commandments. It is therefore God's compassionate grace that forgives sin, and it is his *ḥesed* and *emeth* that characterize his relationship to the forgiven community. Perhaps we may see this same order of *ḥen* and *hesed* in the psalmist's prayer for pardon: "Show me *hen*, O God, according to thy *hesed*, according to the abundance of thy compassion blot out my transgression" (51:3 [1]). In another psalm the order is that the LORD forgives all iniquities and heals all diseases, and then he crowns with *hesed* and compassion (103:3-4).

In assessing the data of the Old Testament the interpreter may on the one hand yield to the temptation of making distinctions where none really exists, or on the other hand may become insensitive and fail to catch the instructive variations within Scripture. Further we need to be repeatedly warned against setting words and phrases within neatly defined categories. Biblical scholars know well that the living word of prophet and psalmist breaks out of our well-intended definitions, so that it is constantly necessary to listen carefully to what the Scripture intends to communicate through its use of words and phrases. With some diffidence therefore we make the following summary: The LORD demonstrated his grace in choosing Israel to be his people with whom he established his covenant, further he graciously forgave the sin of his wayward people, and in that setting he continually performed *hesed* and *emeth* to manifest his faithful covenantal loyalty to his people.

Israel's Response

A brief comment about Israel's response to the *hesed* received from the LORD should be made here. The well-known response, as given in Deuteronomy 6:5, requires Israel to love God with

173

all her heart and soul and might. The prophet Hosea, however, describes the sought-for response as Israel's *ḥesed* toward God. At the outset this prophet declares that the LORD will betroth rebellious Israel to him in righteousness, in justice, in compassion, in *ḥesed,* and in *emunah.* This divine *ḥesed,* as A. Weiser says in his commentary, is not an impulsive mood but the basis of a personal fellowship between God and people.[10] However, in his contention with the people of the land, God found no *ḥesed* and *emeth,* no faithful love toward God and toward man (Hos. 4:1). If there were any *ḥesed,* it evaporated like the morning cloud (6:4). The relationship between God and people was not to be built on sacrifice but on *ḥesed,* not on ceremony but on the knowledge of God (6:6). It is *ḥesed* and justice that repentant Israel must manifest. Gomer, the wayward wife of Hosea, represented the infidelity and unfaithfulness of Israel, her lack of *ḥesed.* In her restored state Israel was to display her faithful love for God and his people.

It is interesting to note that Jeremiah, who was greatly influenced by Hosea, employed his predecessor's word to picture Israel in her ideal time in the wilderness: "Thus says the LORD, I remember the *ḥesed* of your youth, your love as a bride, how you followed me in the wilderness, in a land not sown" (Jer. 2:2). At that time Israel responded to the LORD, her husband, in loyal devotion and love. The point to be remembered here is that Israel made her response by manifesting *ḥesed.*

174

Summary

1. *Hesed* and *emeth* are related words often used in combination to describe a relationship of steadfastness, loyalty, and faithfulness. *Hesed* is the more prominent of the two, and *emeth* is sometimes added to enforce the meaning of faithfulness.

2. Within the covenant which the LORD established with Israel he maintains this relationship in *hesed* and *emeth* so that these words tend to become synonyms of "covenant" (cf. Ps. 89).

3. *Hesed* may be regarded as an expected favor within a relationship, and *hen* as an unmerited favor which a superior bestows on an inferior. Thus the LORD established his covenant because of *hen,* and forgave sin to restore Israel into the covenantal relationship.

4. The response which Israel should make, according to Hosea, is to manifest *hesed* to the LORD and to his people.[11]

John's Prologue

At the beginning of this chapter attention was called to the evangelist's testimony about the Word, "And the Word became flesh and dwelt among us, full of grace and truth" (Jn. 1:14). It seems most reasonable to believe that the Old Testament words which were used to describe the LORD God of Israel are here ascribed to Jesus, thereby attesting to his deity. What was said of God in the Old Testament is here said to be equally true of Jesus of Nazareth. The prologue as-

175

serts further that the law was given through Moses;
grace and truth came through Jesus Christ. This is
to say that the God full of grace and truth revealed
through the law had now fully come in Jesus
Christ, who was indeed full of grace and truth, and
of that fullness all had received grace upon grace.
Even as in the Old Testament God's covenantal
faithfulness was bestowed to Israel time upon time,
so also within the first generation of Christian believers God's faithful redemptive grace in Christ
came time upon time.

It is significant to note that the word "grace,"
charis, occurs four times in verses 14-17 and does
not appear again in the rest of the gospel. It is
twice used with "truth," "full of grace and truth."
"Truth" is used some twenty-five times in this gospel, and one wonders why the word "grace" was
dropped. A plausible answer may be that the evangelist abandons the word, for he intends to let the
word "truth" carry the full import of the concept
within the expression "grace and truth." This is to
say, John would let "truth" become the word to
declare that God's faithfulness to his covenant of
redemption has become manifest in Jesus who declared, "I am the way, and the truth, and the life"
(14:6). Truth, as understood in Old Testament usage, has now become incarnate in Jesus of Nazareth.[12]

But we may well ask the question which C. H.
Dodd raises. Did those who read the gospel, or
those who heard it read, understand *alêtheia* to
mean that which *emeth* meant in the Old Testament? Or what was the common understanding of

176

alêtheia among people using Greek in the first century?[13] In the literature of the time the word had the fundamental meaning of the real as against the unreal, the actual as against the apparent, the true as against the false. One can here sense a difference between the Hebrew and Greek concepts of truth. If the Greek spoke of the true God it would be in contrast to a false God. In the Old Testament truth or *emeth* as it relates to God would speak about the faithfulness and reliability of God. Psalm 25:5, according to LXX, reads, "Lead me in thy truth," but a more accurate rendering of the Hebrew would be, "Lead me through thy faithfulness." The Greek *alêtheia* is something abstract, a concept of the mind; the Old Testament *emeth* is a God-man relationship manifesting faithfulness.

We should readily accede to the conclusions of New Testament scholars of repute, such as Dodd, Strachan, and Barrett, to mention just a few, that the Greek sense of the real, the genuine, or the truthful is to be found in passages such as "I am the true vine" (15:1) ; "For my flesh is the true bread and my blood is the true drink" (6:55) ; or in Jesus' word to the woman at the well, "He whom you now have is not your husband; this you said truthfully" (4:18) .[14] And others can be added.

However, there appears to be a consensus among scholars that in this gospel there is a fusing of the Hebrew idea of *emeth* with the Greek concept of *alêtheia*. It is not difficult to detect concepts of faithfulness or dependability in some passages of this gospel. Let us observe a few. "He who does what is true comes to the light" (3:21) .

177

This indicates the practice of fidelity and steadfastness. Also, the Spirit is called the Spirit of truth. He is to be the manifestation of Jesus who has ascended into heaven. If we may equate the fullness of grace and truth in Jesus with the redemptive faithfulness of God in sending his Son to save the world, then the Spirit of truth is to lead the disciples into that redemptive faithfulness of God (16:13). This is to say that the disciples will time upon time and in increasing measure receive and experience the gracious faithfulness of God's redemption. In this setting Jesus declared, "All that the Father has is mine; therefore I said that he will take what is mine and declare it to you" (16:15). If all that the Father has may be compressed into the prologue statement "full of grace and truth," then it is clear that the Spirit of truth would take this fullness of God, this faithful redeeming action, so abundantly demonstrated in the Old Testament, and he would lead the disciples into this.

Sanctified in Truth

In the intercessory prayer of Christ we have truth related to being sanctified.

> Sanctify them in the truth; thy word is truth. As thou didst send me into the world, so I have sent them into the world. And for their sake I sanctify myself, that they also may be sanctified in truth (17:17-19).

Two concepts in this passage require our attention. They are to be found in the words "sanc-

178

tify" and "truth." The word "sanctify" (make holy) has the basic sense of separation, especially from the profane world for service for God. Since Jesus has already declared in this prayer that the disciples are not of the world, for the world has hated them (17:14), it would seem that here "sanctify" would carry some additional concept, such as faithful devotion to or perseverance in their mission. Here the burden of Jesus' prayer is a concern for the disciples already called and chosen by him, that they would remain dedicated to their mission in the hostile world. Thus it appears that here "sanctify" denotes separation for faithful service.

The second concept is to be derived from the word "truth." If we have correctly discerned the Old Testament understanding of this word as descriptive of faithfulness in all relationships with God and with man, and if "truth" in this gospel often incorporates this Old Testament sense, then we have something other than the Greek concept of the real, the genuine, or the verifiable. This truth, as we have noted above, embodies the faithfulness and dependability of God which he has manifested in Jesus Christ, his Son, and which is to be communicated through Jesus to his disciples. This indeed is what the Spirit of truth would do as he presents the gifts of Christ to the disciples. To be consecrated or to be sanctified through the truth, therefore, is to possess steadfast devotion by means of the steadfastness of God communicated through Jesus Christ.

This interpretation finds support from verse

19 where Jesus declares, "For their sakes I sanctify myself that they also may be sanctified in truth." Here, as above, the word "sanctify" implies more than the idea of separation for a task. Jesus expresses faithfulness to the mission for which he came, which includes his suffering and death. For the sake of his disciples he now sanctifies himself to finish that mission for which he was sent into the world. This act of self-dedication as expressed by Jesus has one purpose, that the disciples may also be dedicated in truth. What Jesus manifested in his faithfulness to do the Father's will would be the pattern of the faithful dedication of the disciples. This would be in truth, that is, in persevering steadfastness.

What is Truth?

We shall close this study about "truth" with the evangelist John's significant use of this interesting word. This occurs when Jesus stands before Pilate. In summary, the conversation between Pilate and Jesus is about being the King of the Jews. Jesus assures Pilate that his kingship is not of this world. If it were, his servants would fight for him.

> Pilate said to him, "So you are a king?" Jesus answered, "You say that I am a king. For this I was born, and for this I have come into the world, to bear witness to the truth. Every one who is of the truth hears my voice." Pilate said to him, "What is truth?" (18:37-38).

It seems very likely that the evangelist has more in mind than recording some conversation between Jesus and Pilate during the trial. The evangelist's method, throughout his gospel, is to present his primary purpose, not in the sign or the event or conversation as such, but in what the sign or event or conversation represents for understanding Christ in his suffering and glorification. So in this instance the conversation's special point of emphasis concerns truth. And the special emphasis involves the unique difference between the Old Testament or Hebrew understanding of "truth" and the Greek-Roman understanding of that word. In the presence of Pilate Jesus declares that his main purpose for being born and coming into the world is to bear witness to the truth, to the truth of God which he himself is in fullness, even as the prologue states. This truth incorporates God's faithfulness, God's redemption, and God's grace which is seen in his redemptive faithfulness. This is the truth that confronts the world. Primarily it confronts the Jews, but it also confronts the Greeks. There had been Greeks who wanted to see Jesus. There were other sheep who were not of this fold. And did not the prologue say that this Jesus was the true light that enlightens every man that comes into the world? This emphasis reaches its climax in the conversation with Pilate. Jesus asserts that in himself God manifests truth, and further that every one who is of the truth hears and obeys his voice.

The phrase "every one who is of the truth" designates those, often referred to in this gospel, who have been wondrously brought within the kingdom of God (3:3-7), and have from his

181

fullness received grace upon grace (1:16).[15] They have come within the redemptive act of God as demonstrated in Jesus Christ. Since they are of God they readily respond in obedience to Jesus, who is the truth of God.

Jesus' declaration about truth made little sense to Pilate, because in his mind the word "truth" carried the commonly accepted Greek-Roman concepts. It is hard to determine the mind of Pilate at this point, but there is something of either disdain or bewilderment in his reply. It is clear that his question had no bearing on his verdict, "I find no crime in him." If this conversation between Jesus and Pilate had no bearing on the trial, then we may inquire why the evangelist incorporated it. His intent, apparently, is to place Jesus, the fullness of truth, over against Pilate, who represented the ideas of truth of the Greek-Roman world. Salvation-truth is not to be found in Greek-Roman systems of culture or law, not in truth as they understood it. Rather, salvation-truth is incarnated in Jesus; and it is through him that salvation-truth becomes redemption for the world. At the beginning of his gospel the evangelist has posted his thesis, "the Word became flesh and dwelt among us, full of grace and truth" (1:14) ; at the close of the gospel this truth confronts the world.

Let us conclude this chapter at this focal point where our three words, *hen,* unmerited grace, *hesed,* steadfast love, and *emeth,* faithfulness, converge upon the Gentile world represented by Pilate. These words are more than concepts. They describe the faithful and redemptive act of God as demonstrated in Christ. He, as our evangelist declared, is the truth. The pathos of this incident is that the Gentile world, with its notion of truth, turned aside. We ought not to miss the evangelist's point that the world, with its truth, will constantly turn aside. Yet Jesus came to present the truth, the truth in all of its Old Testament meaning, to Pilate, to the Gentile world. And he declared that everyone who is of the truth hears and obeys his voice. So then before the Pilates, before the Gentiles, and before the Jews, we who are of this truth take for ourselves the appropriate word of Jesus: "For this I was born, and for this I came into the world, to bear witness to the truth."

NOTES

1. The Hebrew words are *rab ḥesed wemeth*, which the R.S.V. renders "abounding in steadfast love and faithfulness," the A.S.V., "abundant in lovingkindness and truth," and the K.J.V., "abundant in goodness and truth." The LXX reads *polueleos kai alêthinos*, "of much mercy and truth." The evangelist has *plêrês charitos kai alêtheias*, "full of grace and truth." It will be noted that in both the LXX and the New Testament the Hebrew *emeth* is rendered with the same Greek root *alêtheia: ḥesed* receives *eleos* most often in the LXX, but in later Greek *charis* became more popular and apparently supplanted *eleos* in rendering the Hebrew *ḥesed*. This may explain the variation between the LXX and John 1:14.

2. Nelson Glueck, *Das Wort Hesed im alttestament-*

liche Sprachgebrauch (Giessen: A. Töpelmann, 1927).
English Translation *Hesed in the Bible* (Cincinnati:
The Hebrew Union College Press, 1967).

3. **Cf.** Gen. 21:23; Judg. 1:24; 8:35; I Sam. 20:8, 14-15; II Sam. 2:5; 3:8; 16:17.

4. Lofthouse, "*Hen and Hesed* in the Old Testament," *Zeitschrift für die Alttestamentliche Wissenschaft* (1933), pp. 29-35.

5. A comparison is here given of four English versions, the New Dutch version, the Zürich version, and the new Jerusalem version:

Ex. 34:6	K.J.V.	abundant in goodness and truth
	E.S.V.	plenteous in mercy and truth
	A.S.V.	abundant in lovingkindness and truth
	R.S.V.	abounding in steadfast love and faithfulness
	N.D.	*groot van goedertierenheid en trouw*
	Zür.	*reich an Huld und Treue*
	Jer.	rich in kindness and faithfulness
Ps. 25:10	K.J.V.	all the paths of the Lord are mercy and truth
	E.S.V.	and A.S.V.—lovingkindness and truth
	R.S.V.	steadfast love and faithfulness
	N.D.	*goedertierenheid en trouw*
	Zür.	*Huld und Treue*
	Jer.	love and truth

6. O. Procksch, *Theologie des Alten Testaments* (Gütersloh: C. Bertelsmann Verlag, 1950), p. 606.

7. To the anointed one God manifests his *hesed*; Ps. 18:51 [50]; II Sam. 22:51.

8. Glueck, *op. cit.*, pp. 42-43 (ET pp. 75-79). It is this same normative faithful relationship of God which Solomon noted on taking the throne as David's son; I Kings 3:6; II Chron. 1:8.

9. *Ibid.*, pp. 51-52 (ET pp. 87-88).

10. A. Weiser, *Das Buch der zwölf Kleinen*

Propheten, "Das Alte Testament Deutsch" (Göttingen: Vandenhoeck & Ruprecht, 1956), p. 33.

11. The conclusion reached in the above study of *hesed* unfortunately does not satisfy every instance of its use. This note takes up one of those instances, which is the well-known text of Isaiah 40:6, "Hark, one is saying, 'Cry!' And I said, 'What shall I cry?' All flesh is grass and all its *hesed* [*hasdo,* Hebrew text] is like the flower of the field." Faithful love or covenantal loyalty does not offer good sense here since neither quality is found in the flower of the field with which a comparison is made. Most translators have followed the LXX's *doxa,* the only instance of its use for *hesed.* **Cf.** the Vulgate's *gloria,* the K.J.V.'s "goodliness," the R.S.V.'s "beauty." Apparently the idea of glory derives from the comparison with the flower of the field, but it poorly serves the other object of the comparison, all flesh. **Emendations** such as *kebodo, hedaro,* or *hodo* (its glory, its beauty, or its splendor) have been offered to justify the translation "glory."

My study of the above passage leads me to the conclusion that in this instance and in certain psalms *hesed* means "strength," which would yield the following: "All flesh is grass and all its strength is as the flower of the field." **Cf.** *Vetus Testamentum,* Vol. XIII (1963), pp. 489-92; *Reformed Review,* Vol. 16 (1962), p. 11, n. 13.

12. In surveying some of the extensive literature on the meaning of "truth" in the Gospel of John one does not find a consensus among scholars. Perhaps the closest approach to agreement is that in the Johannine literature "truth" embraces something of the Old Testament idea of God's faithfulness which is revealed in the Word made flesh. R. Bultmann asserts that truth is the divine reality revealed in Jesus Christ. The acceptance of this truth-revelation results in salvation and eternal life; "Alêtheia," *Theological Dictionary of the New Testament,* ed. G. Kittel, I (1964), pp. 245-47. O. A. Piper declares that when Jesus affirms that God is true (Jn.

3:33) he is saying that God acts in accordance with his established relationship with a sinful world. Piper finds that in John's Gospel truth has intrinsic energy to make itself known, whereas in the Old Testament it has the emphasis of God's being unchangeable, a quality of God seen in the salvation plan in the history of Israel which is actualized in Jesus; "Truth," *The Interpreter's Dictionary of the Bible,* ed. G. A. Buttrick, R-Z (1962), pp. 715-16. J. H. Vrielink, after his study of *emeth* in the Old Testament yields the interpretation of faithfulness and dependability, states that "truth" in John's Gospel carries the connotation of "to be-out-of-God," *uit-God zijn.* This is a relationship of faithfulness which offers freedom and life; *Het Waarheidsbegrip* (Nijkerk: G. F. Callenbach N. V., 1956) , pp. 81-102.

13. C. H. Dodd, *The Fourth Gospel* (Cambridge: The University Press, 1953) , pp. 170-78.

14. C. H. Dodd, *op. cit.*; R. H. Strachan, *The Fourth Gospel* (London: SCM Press, 1941) ; C. K. Barrett, *The Gospel According to St. John* (London: SPCK, 1955) .

15. Other designations are: "Born . . . of God" (1:13) , "one born anew" (3:3) , "one born of water and the Spirit" (3:5-6) , "every one who has heard and learned from the Father" (6:45) , "he who is of God" (8:47) .

CHAPTER VII

THE PROBLEM
OF SUFFERING

> How long, O LORD? Wilt thou forget me for ever?
> How long wilt thou hide thy face from me?
> How long must I bear pain in my soul,
> and have sorrow in my heart all the day?
> How long shall my enemy be exalted over me?
> (Ps. 13:1-2).

THE CHURCH COMMONLY USES THE BOOK OF Psalms to express praise and thanksgiving to God, even as Israel once did. Many psalms lend themselves to this purpose; the selection is not restricted to a few. However, the psalter contains other types of psalms which have not come into general usage because they seem less suitable for Christians at worship. Psalms like the one above are known as laments, and express the psalmist's great heaviness of spirit because of misfortune or the taunts of his enemy. Others, like the laments, are psalms that call for God's vindication against accusers (7, 17, 26). And some psalmists pour out prayers of imprecation, asking God to rise in wrath and bring destruction upon their enemies (69, 109, 137). To the church which has been instructed in the gospel of love and forgiveness these psalms have not appeared quite acceptable and have consequently been little used.

Yet a sizable portion of Israel's literature contains laments and complaints of various kinds. The Chronicler noted that Jeremiah uttered a lament at the death of King Josiah and that a guild for making laments continued even to the time of the author (II Chron. 35:25). It may well be that lament writers were a certain group of poets and singers who claimed Jeremiah as the founder of their guild, much like the wisemen who considered Solomon as the founder of the wisdom school, and like the poets who regarded David as the chief psalmist in Israel. Since laments were set in poetic forms it would follow that many would appear in the Psalms. However, the problems raised in the cries of anguish and distress were also known to prophets and especially to wisemen who considered the problems that arose in life, and we find the burden of Israel raised and pondered in several books of the Old Testament.

To understand their burden we must bear in mind that all these Old Testament writers stood within the covenant community in which they had learned about the redemptive acts of the LORD who had brought Israel out of her bondage to make her his covenant people. In this relationship to the LORD Israel was confronted with the choice of good and evil, to keep the commandments or to become disobedient. The obedient people would receive God's blessing on their labors, but the disobedient would come under the wrath of God, which would bring calamity and evil upon them. In line with this teaching, when Israel's writers observed that God sent his favor upon the godly and his judgment upon the wicked there was no burden of soul and no lament needed to be spoken. If, however, the accepted formula of God's justice and his wrath could not be discerned, consternation and questioning would arise and it was expressed in laments.

The Solidarity Concept

In our concern for justice for the individual, we need to be reminded that in Israel the tribe or the nation was considered a unit and consequently the tribe or nation shared in the merit or guilt of individuals within itself. This is known as the solidarity concept and helps us to see why in some instances God's favor rested upon those who were unworthy, and why judgment came upon those not guilty.

Let us cite some examples of the solidarity concept. Abraham addressed his intercession to the LORD for the welfare of Sodom with this rhetorical question, "Shall not the Judge of all the earth do right?" (Gen. 18:25). The implied answer was the basis for Abraham's intercession. "To do right" as expressed in the prayer was not to "slay the righteous with the wicked, so that the righteous fare as the wicked," and to spare Sodom herself for the sake of the few, the ten righteous. The merit of the few righteous became an accepted dogma in Israel. Ezekiel, however, protested against it since it suggested a false security against the coming judgment of God. The prophet pronounced his doom as follows: "Even if these three men, Noah, Daniel, and Job, were in it, they would deliver but their own lives by their righteousness" (Ezek. 14:14, cf. ver. 20). The dogma had been pressed too far and had become a spurious guarantee against any disaster. A further illustration of the merit of the righteous can be seen in the case of David, whose uprightness was remembered by the LORD in the generations after David's rule, for the LORD did not send the evil upon the disobedient descendants of David because he remembered that David had done right in the eyes of the LORD (I Kings 15:2-5; II Kings 8:18-19).

Conversely, though, the concept of solidarity also meant that the sin and guilt of one or a few could become the guilt of the tribe and the cause of disaster. Because of Achan's sin in taking the consecrated booty of Jericho the army of Israel suffered a serious defeat at Ai (Josh. 7). After Achan and his family had been destroyed and the guilt thereby removed from Israel, the people fought successfully against Ai (ch. 8). Because of the blood guilt on the house of Saul because he put Gibeonites to death, a three-year famine came upon Israel (II Sam. 21:1). David's sin of numbering the people of Israel resulted in the LORD's sending a pestilence upon Israel (II Sam. 24:15). Job protested vehemently against the accepted dogma that the sons of the wicked should suffer the punishment which their fathers escaped (Job 21:19-21). The phrase of the second commandment, "visiting the iniquity of the fathers upon the

190

children to the third and the fourth generation of those who hate me" (Ex. 20:5), had become formalized into a maxim, "The fathers have eaten sour grapes, and the children's teeth are set on edge" (Jer. 31:29; Ezek. 18:2). The prophets called this into question as they taught that the individual was responsible for his own conduct, and would not be held responsible for the sins of the fathers. The protest is also heard in Deuteronomy, "The fathers shall not be put to death for the children, nor shall the children be put to death for the fathers; every man shall be put to death for his own sin" (24:16; cf. II Kings 14:6).

Jeremiah's and Ezekiel's preaching against the collectivism in the saying concerning the fathers eating sour grapes established the point that "every one shall die for his own sin: each man who eats sour grapes, his teeth shall be set on edge" (Jer. 31:30). This meant that the LORD's justice was vindicated in that he would give to each what he deserved. Ezekiel thereby rebuked the charge current in the talk of Israel, "The way of the Lord is not just" (Ezek. 18:25, 29), for the LORD gives to each his due. It was rather the ways of Israel that were not just, and therefore God's doom had come upon her. The old formula of God's justice which brought reward and retribution was not abandoned; it was made to apply to the individual apart from any collective merit or guilt.

As Israel encountered the experiences in life, her prophets, poets, and wisemen could not but observe that the formula of the LORD's even-handed justice could not be detected in all instances. Thus

191

laments were not only voiced by psalmists as we noted above, but much serious reflection was given to the apparent injustices and inequities encountered by the pious in Israel. Our purpose will be to follow the thought of these Old Testament writers as, in their faith based upon God who had revealed himself as just, merciful, and faithful, they came to know why God's people were subjected to misfortune and evil.

Suffering is Disciplinary

The psalmist (Ps. 119), whose chief delight was in the revelation of the LORD given through his law and word, nevertheless declares that he has become the scorn of the insolent (ver. 22), that princes are plotting against him (ver. 23), and that his soul cleaves to the dust (ver. 25). He further states that he is ensnared by the cords of the wicked (ver. 61), that he is slandered and put to shame (ver. 69, 78), and that he is being persecuted with falsehood (ver. 86), so that he utters the lament, "How long must thy servant endure? When wilt thou judge those who persecute me?" (ver. 84). In the midst of his consternation he observes that affliction had taught him the meaning of God's word. "It is good for me that I was afflicted, that I might learn thy statutes" (ver. 71, cf. also ver. 67).

In Psalm 94 the poet raises this lament, "O LORD, how long shall the wicked, how long shall the wicked exult?" (ver. 3). In answer to this complaint, he reflects on the living presence of God who hears and sees and chastens not only nations but also the godly one so that he may be instructed by the law and gain a new perspective in time of trouble (ver. 12).

In their dialogue with Job his friends use God's discipline as an explanation for his affliction. Eliphaz declares that the Almighty's chastening will be the occasion for God to show his healing and redeeming power (Job 5:17-20). Elihu more pointedly asserts that in affliction God makes man's transgression known to him in order to teach him to repent (36:9-10). The godless do not profit from their affliction, but the godly are delivered from it, for they heed the instruction and repent, and as a consequence receive the favor of God (36:13-16). It is noteworthy that nowhere in the dialogue does Job refute this argument about the disciplinary purpose of affliction and this may be a subtle and tacit recognition of its validity, in that Job, through his affliction, comes to a new understanding of God. God had indeed opened Job's ear through adversity.

The writer of Proverbs sets forth the discipline of the LORD through the figure of a father's loving concern for the son he disciplines:

> My son, do not despise the LORD's discipline
> or be weary of his reproof,
> for the LORD reproves him whom he loves,
> as a father the son in whom he delights (3:11-12).

The author of Hebrews found this passage especially suitable for admonishing Christians perplexed about their affliction, pointing out the benefits of

193

receiving discipline from God their Father (Heb. 12:5-11).

Suffering Reveals Genuine Faith

The prologue of the book of Job raises the question whether disinterested piety exists in the world. Satan, whose name means the adversary, appears before God and his heavenly council to allege that genuine piety cannot be produced upon earth. In his going to and fro on the earth and up and down in it he has observed the conduct of people. This leads the LORD to ask whether Satan has observed Job, who lives above the level of many in the world, in his maturity, his uprightness, his reverence for God, and his avoidance of evil. Satan calls the virtue of Job into question with these words, "Does Job fear God for naught?" (1:9). Satan asserts that Job's goodness and piety rests upon the rewards which God has lavishly given. If rewards would be withheld, Job would renounce God to his face.

Satan's challenge to put the piety of Job to the test is accepted. Afflictions come upon Job in rapid succession. The man of wealth becomes the man of poverty; the man with a family of children becomes childless; the man of sound health becomes a victim of a loathsome disease which covers his body with sores; and the man who enjoyed popular esteem in the city gate becomes the despised man sitting on the ash heap. His wife, his only remaining source of comfort, becomes a mouthpiece for Satan in saying, "Do you still hold fast your integrity? Curse God and die" (2:9). The test to prove Job's integrity or maturity is thorough and complete. Will a man keep his piety and maturity, manifested by uprightness and kindness in life, when calamity and affliction come upon him?

The answer to Satan's challenge is to come from the mouth of Job, for Satan said that Job would curse God to his face. However, Job's first response is submission and praise. "Naked I came from my mother's womb, and naked shall I return; the LORD gave, and the LORD has taken away; blessed be the name of the LORD" (1:21). The second response made in answer to his wife's counsel of despair is, "You speak as one of the foolish women would speak. Shall we receive good at the hand of God, and shall we not receive evil?" (2:10), in which Job declares that both prosperity and calamity are dispensed by God in this world. Therefore it would be foolish, a sign of spiritual immaturity, to renounce God when calamity comes. Since good and evil do exist in the world which God has established, one must expect both the good and the evil as normative in the experience of life. Neither the one nor the other should determine piety and moral uprightness.

The author adds two comments which support the conclusion that Job had met the test successfully and that God's evaluation of Job was vindicated: "In all this Job did not sin or charge God with wrong" (1:22), and "In all this Job did not sin with his lips" (2:10).

The intended conclusion of the prologue is that genuine piety does and can exist without compensating rewards. Or to state the conclusion differently, affliction upon the godly can demonstrate their spiritual maturity and genuine piety.

One of the significant words in this narrative heads the list of adjectives that describe the character of Job, It is *tam*, which is rendered "blameless" by the R.S.V. and "perfect" by the K.J.V. (1:1, 8; 2:3). Of the four adjectives used, only this one appears in nounal form in two important places in the story. The first instance is in the second conversation with Satan where the LORD says, "He still holds fast his integrity [*tummathô*], although you moved me against him, to destroy him without cause" (2:3). The second use is by Job's wife who asks, "Do you still hold fast your integrity [*tummathekha*]? Curse God and die" (2:9). The meaning of this root suggests being fully developed, being ripe or full grown, or being mature. The descriptive quality which we shall call maturity was being put to the test as afflictions came upon Job.

The intended conclusion of the prologue makes clear that Job did in truth have that kind of maturity which kept him from opening his mouth to denounce God, as Satan alleged that he would do. Both God and Job's wife observe that he held fast to his integrity, his spiritual maturity, and thus demonstrated that genuine piety does and can exist without compensating rewards.

In the sermon on the mount Jesus elaborated on the theme of going beyond the common practice of doing good only to those from whom one expects favor in return. The basis for this teaching is "You, therefore, must be perfect, as your heavenly Father is perfect" (Mt. 5:48). The adjective "perfect" *(teleios)* is frequently used in the LXX for rendering the Hebrew *tam,* which suggests that the Greek adjective carries with it the concept of being fully developed or mature, even as the R.S.V. renders it in some places (**cf.** Eph. 4:13; Phil. 3:15). Even though "perfect" seems more felicitous as a description of God, "mature" rather happily describes the "sons of your Father who is in heaven" (5:45).

Jesus' teaching urges those who are his disciples to manifest their spiritual maturity by doing good to those from whom no return is expected. The mature disciple will practice this type of goodness because he has achieved this ideal by observing that his Father in heaven bestows his blessing upon all people, the just and the unjust.

Jesus' teaching and the prologue of Job both emphasize the excellence of a mature piety. In the prologue this maturity is evidenced by a person's response to affliction; according to the teaching of Jesus by one's observing the unrestricted goodness of God.

Suffering Enriches Fellowship with God

The prologue of Job clearly vindicates God's high esteem of Job against Satan's cynical attack. Satan's charge that piety and moral living must have rewards to exist is proven false. Job keeps his spiritual maturity in the face of extreme and bewildering afflictions. The author, however, intends the prologue to do more than vindicate God's confidence in Job, for he brings Job's three friends to engage Job in a long and intense debate on the problem of suffering. Neither Job nor the friends appear to be aware of the conclusion reached in the prologue. Rather, introducing the friends into the narrative initiates the dialogue about the purpose of suffering, a problem which perplexed many godly in Israel, and was expressed in the well-known words of the psalmist, "My God, my God, why hast thou forsaken me?" (Ps. 22:2 [1]).

In the presence of his friends Job begins the conversation by cursing the day of his birth (ch. 3). Since his suffering is severe, and since no light comes to illumine the dark mystery of his grievous affliction, life has lost purpose and it seems better not to have been born (cf. Jer. 20:14-18). The friends, each in their turn, expound the accepted dogma of rewards and retributions by which God punishes the wicked but sends his favor upon the godly. Eliphaz claims that he has received from God a revelation that mortal man is not pure and therefore should not question the way of God (4:12ff.). Bildad appeals to the past to point out that God has always rejected the evil man, but has accepted the godly (8:8-22). Zophar asserts that man, limited in understanding, should not hope to comprehend the mysteries of God (ch. 11). The friends frequently urge Job to repent of his sins, for if he does so God will again restore him to his former prosperity. And as Job continues vehemently to maintain his innocence, the friends point to his obvious pride or lack of humility before God, and to his insensitivity to his own evil which, if he were to acknowledge it, would restore him into the favor of God. Throughout the dialogue they contend that God's justice is being manifested, and therefore Job must be receiving just recompense for his sins.

Job severely attacks his friends for their insensitivity both to his suffering and to his perplexity about the cause for all his anguish. Since Job labors with the same doctrine of reward and retribution which the friends are propounding, he is greatly perplexed because he can find in his life no sin so heinous or abominable that it would warrant the intensity of his agony. Since he finds no answer for his problem in the speeches of the friends, he turns to God and asks that God make clear to him the reason for his distress. But alas, God does not answer, at least not at first. Then, in frantic desperation, Job wants a vindication of his innocence to be recorded, perhaps inscribed upon a rock, so that future generations may know the truth about him. As though this vindication is not enough, Job appeals to God to be his Vindicator in the well-known passage, "For I know that my Redeemer lives" (19:25). This vindication will be in the after time, for Job has no hope of recovery to enjoy vindication now. However, after his flesh has been destroyed, then he shall see God on his side as his Redeemer and Vindicator (19:25-27).

This vindication by God in the life to come does not prove to be the solution the author has in mind, for the dialogue continues, although with less intensity than at first. Throughout the dialogue both Job and the friends are seeking an answer to the question of why the righteous should have affliction in the context of the traditional dogma of God's blessing the righteous and sending affliction upon the wicked. Job stands upon this tradition and from this point of view demands an answer from God.

After much waiting God finally does answer in what is known as the LORD's speech from the whirlwind (ch. 38-41). He confronts Job with the wonderful acts of creation about which Job has no knowledge. Further, Job is asked to contemplate the forces of nature: light, snow, rain, clouds, and various animals such as the lion, the mountain goat, the wild ass, the ostrich, and the horse. Job is then asked how *he* would rule the affairs of men. Finally he is called to consider two monsters of ancient time, possibly the hippopotamus and the crocodile, which are described in terms of horror and wonder. The effect of describing all these wonders of nature is that Job cannot grasp the meaning of what he has seen and is left with a sense of the incomprehensible mystery of the world about him:

> Behold, I am of small account;
> what shall I answer thee?
> I lay my hand on my mouth.
> I have spoken once, and I will not answer;
> twice, but I will proceed no further (40:4-5).
> Therefore I have uttered what I did not understand,
> things too wonderful for me, which I did not know (42:3).

200

We should note that the LORD's speech from the whirlwind does not answer Job's question about his affliction; neither does it vindicate Job and rebuke the friends as a reader might expect. Rather, the speech confronts Job with an incomprehensible mystery in the natural world, a mystery beyond the understanding of man. The intended parallel to the moral world of justice, rewards, and retributions is not difficult to detect. To state it plainly, if indeed the world of nature is an incomprehensible mystery, how much more the world of moral law and justice. Both are beyond human understanding.

The speech from the whirlwind prepares Job to make the great utterance which is the grand climax to the lengthy dialogue about the mystery of suffering.

> I had heard of thee by the hearing of the ear,
> but now my eye sees thee;
> therefore I reject my words,[1]
> and repent in dust and ashes (42:5-6) .

In this short saying Job contrasts what he formerly believed about God according to the traditional teaching with what he now knows God to be. He now sees that he was wrong to demand an answer from God from his stance within the framework of traditional dogma, that which had come to him "by the hearing of the ear." His eye now sees God in another view, a view which does not end in an incomprehensible mystery. He now understands God to be gracious love, especially to those afflicted, whose relationship to God must not be sought in terms of justice and rewards but in manifesta-

201

tions of free and overflowing grace. No longer need Job be haunted by the fear of an angry deity or of an irrational demonic power. In his affliction he has reached a new understanding of fellowship with God, which was unknown to him in the days of prosperity. Indeed affliction enhances the fullness of fellowship with God.

The poet in Psalm 73 confronted one of the factors in the problem of suffering debated in Job, the prosperity of the wicked (ver. 3). This poet was troubled because of the success and welfare of the ungodly who arrogantly mocked God (ver. 11-12). He sought relief for his perplexity through devout and upright conduct, but to no avail (ver. 13); and his searching for an answer proved to be "a wearisome task" (ver. 16). Although, while in worship of God in the sanctuary, he discovered that the wicked were "in slippery places," yet his main relief from his burden was to experience a fellowship with God which overcame his bitterness of soul, as he found his highest good in realizing that God was continually near him:

> Nevertheless I am continually with thee;
> thou dost hold my right hand.
> Thou dost guide me with thy counsel,
> and afterward thou wilt receive me to glory.
> Whom have I in heaven but thee?
> And there is nothing upon earth that I desire besides thee.
> My flesh and my heart may fail,
> but God is the strength of my heart and my portion for ever (ver. 23-26).

Thus in his distress and perplexity, this psalmist,

much like Job, came to a new appreciation of fellowship with God.

Wait and See: God Will Act

The prophet Habakkuk began his message with a lament:

> O Lord, how long shall I cry for help,
> and thou wilt not hear?
> Or cry to thee "Violence!"
> and thou wilt not save? (1:2).

His burden was that violence and wrong were much in evidence within Judah, the people of God, and the law was so weak that justice was perverted.

God answered the prophet's complaint by directing his attention to God's rousing the mighty nation of the Chaldeans to bring punishment and chastisement upon the wicked in Judah. However, as the prophet contemplated the scourge of the Chaldeans, his burden was not allayed, for he saw a wicked power swallow up a nation more righteous than itself (1:13). That mighty nation had no regard for God that it should honor him, for it offered sacrifice to the arms by which it prospered. The prophet's complaint, therefore, raised the problem of the rule of evil in the world. How could it be that a pure and just God would countenance gross violence and wrong in the world?

The prophet made his complaint to learn what God would answer. He was told that the vision which would bring the answer was not for the present but that it would surely come, and that he must wait for it. The man who was not upright would fail, but "the righteous one shall live by his faith" (2:4). This meant that in faithfulness to God the prophet should live in confidence that God would ultimately make justice prevail. He should have patience and "Wait and See."

The same problem is raised in the book of Malachi and a similar answer is given. The people have wearied the LORD by saying:

> Every one who does evil is good in the sight of the LORD, and he delights in them. . . . Where is the God of justice? (2:17).

> It is vain to serve God. What is the good of our keeping his charge or of walking as in mourning before the LORD of hosts? Henceforth we deem the arrogant blessed; evil-doers not only prosper but when they put God to the test they escape (3:14-15).

The answer given to these people is that God has kept in remembrance all those who feared him, and that the time is coming when God will act in their behalf. When that day comes, the arrogant and wicked will be destroyed, but those who fear God's name shall have the sun of righteousness, the symbol of deliverance, shine upon them (3:19-21 [4:1-3]). Therefore let the godly wait and see, for deliverance will come.

Many perplexed psalmists found the answers to their questionings in patient waiting. In Psalm 37 the poet speaks to those fretting because of the prosperity of the wicked. He urges his listeners to be patient, for soon the wicked will be cut off and the godly shall prosper (ver. 9-11; 35-40). This attitude of "hope in God" became the consolation for many in affliction (42:6, 12 [5, 11]; 130:5-8). "Wait and See" became the sustaining comfort that God would send his deliverance:

I believe that I shall see the goodness of the LORD
in the land of the living!
Wait for the LORD;
be strong, and let your heart take courage;
yea, wait for the LORD! (27:13-14).

Patience to endure suffering and the injustices of life is as necessary in the New Testament as in the Old. The writer of the Hebrews appeals to the counsel given Habakkuk to wait and see. In many instances believers had been subjected to hard trials, to public abuse, and to loss of property. The author cites Habakkuk 2:3-4 (LXX version) to encourage endurance to do the will of God. The believer must not be one who "shrinks back" but one who lives by his faith, for it will be those with faith who keep their souls, that is, their proper attitude toward life in its difficulties. The "Wait and See" admonition here does not foresee a return to former prosperity as was often the hope of the "Wait and See" solution in the Old Testament. The New Testament saint is instructed to see his prosperity in terms of personal calm and inner satisfaction that result from a life of faith, for it is by this kind of faith that the righteous shall live (Heb. 10:37-39; cf. I Pet. 3:14-15).

The psalms of lament also offer the "Wait and See" answer to the one in distress. The pattern in which these laments are set involves first of all a heart-stirring complaint declaring that the psalmist can no longer discern God's righteous rule, and then, after some reflection about his plight, the psalmist becomes eloquent with praise, for God has heard his lament and brought deliverance. Thus it is in Psalm 13 where the cry of "How long, O LORD? Wilt thou forget me forever?" (ver. 1) ends in a declaration of praise, "I will sing to the LORD, because he has dealt bountifully with me" (ver. 6). The complaints of being in distress and the cries for help are also heard in other psalms (6, 38, 42-43, 56, 69), in each of which the lament is followed with praise for the saving goodness of the LORD.

The best-known lament, chiefly because of its use by Jesus on the cross, is Psalm 22, which begins thus:

> My God, my God, why hast thou forsaken me?
> Why art thou so far from helping me, from the words of my groaning?
> O my God, I cry by day, but thou dost not answer;
> and by night, but find no rest (ver. 2-3 [1-2]).

Then the psalmist recalls the deliverance God performed for the fathers, he describes the mockery he must endure, and he pleads for the LORD's help (ver. 5-22 [4-21]). After this lament the psalmist offers his testimony of praise in the congregation, for he has learned that in due time God will act to deliver him from his anxiety (ver. 25 [24]).

The laments and descriptions of revilings by enemies are less extreme in Psalm 31, but here also

206

the psalmist speaks of bodily distress and of the scorn of enemies (ver. 10-14 [9-13]). His cry for help is heard, however, for the LORD comes to his aid and sets his feet in a broad place (ver. 8-9 [7-8]). The poet therefore commits his spirit into the hands of God who delivers him (ver. 6 [5]).

A reading of the gospels, especially those portions which narrate the suffering and death of Jesus, readily discloses that Jesus entered the experiences of bodily and spiritual affliction which the godly in Israel endured. It is of special significance that during his intense agony on the cross Jesus uttered the lament of the psalmist, "My God, my God, why hast thou forsaken me?" (Mt. 27:46; Mk. 15:34). Then the sorrows of the Old Testament saints, the pains of body, the revilings of those mocking, and the perplexity plaguing the soul, all found their consummation in Jesus Christ as he spoke one of the laments of the psalms. And it is equally noteworthy that at the close of that agony he selected another psalm to declare that God had in truth sustained and delivered him when he said, "Father, into thy hands I commit my spirit!" (Lk. 23:46).

Suffering is Vicarious

The problem of the righteous enduring affliction receives its most profound solution in the teachings of Deutero-Isaiah, the prophet of the exile. In the setting of Israel's affliction which greatly disturbed the godly so that they expressed themselves in laments before God this prophet declared

207

that the Spirit of the LORD had come upon him
(Is. 61:1) to illumine the dark night of Israel's disgrace and despair. His message was not a lament,
but a new understanding of the purpose of suffering endured by the righteous. This purpose the
prophet unfolded as he set forth the ministry of
the Servant of the LORD.

The identity of the Servant, about which
much has been written, need not be discussed at
length here.[2] Our first impression in reading this
prophecy is that the Servant is Israel:

> But now hear, O Jacob my servant,
> Israel whom I have chosen!
> Thus says the LORD who made you,
> who formed you from the womb and will help
>   you:
> Fear not, O Jacob my servant,
> Jeshurun whom I have chosen (44:1-2; also 41:8-9;
>   43:10; 44:21; 48:20; 49:3).

In the first so-called Servant Song (42:1-4) the
LXX translators inserted—or was this their Hebrew
text?—Israel and Jacob, which indicated their iden-
tification of the Servant.

In his description of the Servant the prophet
was informing the exiled people who they still were.
God had chosen them and had not cast them off
(41:8-9); he had created them to make them his
(43:1); they were to be the LORD's witnesses
(43:10); they were blind and deaf, which indicated
their stubbornness and waywardness because of
which the LORD had placed them in the hands of
the spoiler (42:18-25). Yet God had not forgotten
them, for he would redeem them from Babylon

(43:14), and he would blot out their transgressions (43:25; 44:22).

In the Servant Songs, usually delineated 42:1-4; 49:1-6; 50:4-9; 52:13-53:12, the identity of the Servant seems more to become a person than to describe a people. We of western culture should be alerted to the common practice of Hebrew poets and prophets to shift from one concept to another, so that what appears as people may also come in the form of an individual. We shall find our most satisfying interpretation in a fluidity of description moving from a collective sense to a single person. Thus, Israel as Servant may be incorporated in the individual Servant in whom the ministry of the Servant is fully realized.

A brief summary of the Servant Songs is necessary for us to see the course of the Servant's ministry which led to his suffering. In the first Song (42:1-4), the Servant is endowed by God's Spirit to bring justice or practical religion to all the world. In the second Song (49:1-6), the Servant has his mission from birth to the peoples beyond Israel. Since a mission restricted to Israel would be too small, the Servant shall bring the light of salvation to the ends of the earth. In the third Song (50:4-9), the Servant willingly receives instruction to become a teacher. However, he suffers bodily torment and mockery at the hands of men. Yet the Servant knows that God will vindicate him.

The last Song (52:13-53:12) reveals to us the special purpose for which the Servant came. He is first described in terms of exaltation. Yet when kings and nations shall see his abject appearance they shall be dumbfounded, especially when they learn why the Servant is suffering. The Servant comes from an unpromising origin. And when we, that is, those about him, look at him we are not attracted to him. The Servant has sickness and pain which we, according to the accepted doctrine of reward and retribution, explain as God's punishment for sins he committed. But no! We are wrong, for the Servant is enduring pain and sickness because of our transgressions. The stripes which he received in the former Song are for our welfare, for the LORD has placed our guilt upon him. The Servant willingly and without complaint endures the shameful injustice of men and is put to death. In all this he gives himself as an offering for the guilt of others so that by the knowledge of him the many may be accounted righteous. His suffering and death shall end in a great victory of forgiveness and redemption for many. Through his vicarious suffering the Servant brings redemption to Israel and to the nations. This indeed is the high point in the Old Testament teaching about the suffering of the godly.

The Servant in the New Testament

After Peter's confession at Caesarea Philippi that Jesus was the Messiah, Jesus began to tell his disciples that he would suffer many things at the hands of elders, chief priest, and scribes (Mt. 16:21-23). He thus indicated that he was taking upon himself the ministry of the Suffering Servant. Although Jesus made no clear reference to the Ser-

THE PROBLEM OF SUFFERING

vant here, Peter's rebuking him and the stern reproof with which Jesus answered Peter indicate that both of them were thinking about the Old Testament portrait of the Suffering Servant. Peter, who expressed the popular concept of the Messiah without suffering and humiliation, wanted to make clear that his confession did not include the suffering of the Old Testament Servant. Jesus, however, accepted that mission of the Servant as the important part of his ministry. This, as well as the other expectations of the Old Testament, would come to fulfillment in him.

In answer to the request of the mother of James and John that her sons might be honored in Christ's kingdom, Jesus answered that the purpose of his coming was not to awaken desires for honor and recognition, for he came to serve "and to give his life a ransom for many" (Mt. 20:28). Again there was no direct quoting of the prophets, but Jesus did allude to "serving" and to giving his life for the many, both concepts relating to the Servant in Isaiah 53. At the last Supper Jesus spoke of pouring out his blood for the many for the forgiveness of sins (Mt. 26:28), a remark suggestive of Isaiah 53:11-12. To the two disciples on the way to Emmaus, he made clear that according to the prophets the Messiah should suffer and then enter his glory (Lk. 24:25-26). One cannot but be impressed with the allusions which Jesus made to the ministry of the Suffering Servant. Furthermore, the use of these allusions was especially unique in that thereby Jesus took to himself both the role of the Suffering Servant, a role of humiliation, and

211

the role of the exalted Son of Man which was the popular description of the expected Messiah. The combining of these two roles was completely foreign to the thinking of Jews in their anticipation of the promised Messiah. Here, consequently, we may see a unique relationship between the Old and New Testaments established by the teachings of Jesus. The ministry of the Suffering Servant, begun in the Old Testament, finds its consummation in Jesus, especially at the point of his suffering.

The New Testament writers followed the example of Jesus in that they related him to the Suffering Servant. Again this was done by allusion rather than a formal interpretation of Isaiah 53. The closest thing to a formal interpretation was given by the evangelist Philip in his preaching to the Ethiopian eunuch who inquired about the meaning of Isaiah 53:7-8 (Acts 8:32-35). Peter, encouraging Christians to bear their sufferings, patiently set before them the example of Jesus whose patient suffering he described by freely using excerpts from Isaiah 53 (I Pet. 2:21-25). In the early part of Acts references were made to Jesus with the title "his [God's] servant" (3:13, 26; 4:27, 30) and these appear to be allusions to the Servant of the LORD in Isaiah. When Paul wrote "that Christ died for our sins in accordance with the scriptures, that he was buried, that he was raised on the third day in accordance with the scriptures" (I Cor. 15:3-4), he may have been alluding to the description of the Servant in that passage; it had become so generally accepted in the early church as being fulfilled in Christ that a formal reference, "as it is written," and quoting the Old Testament (as I Cor. 1:19; 2:9; 3:19; 15:45, 54-55) were no longer necessary. Thus we can observe that the New Testament writers, largely by allusions and by their acceptance of the established interpretation, witnessed that Jesus Christ was the fulfillment of the ministry of the Suffering Servant as given in Deutero-Isaiah (cf. further Mt. 8:17; 12:17-21).[3]

The New Testament church regarded herself as the new Israel and significantly took on the role of being the Servant of the LORD. Parallels were made between the church and Israel. The church had also been created by God and chosen by him; the church, even though chosen by God, had sinned and came under the chastisement of God; the church had received the forgiveness of God through Christ; and the church had been redeemed and made to be witnesses of God in the world. The church's importance as witness was expressed by Paul, in a significant appeal to a Servant passage (Is. 49:6), in his decision to preach to the Gentiles: "I have set you to be a light for the Gentiles, that you may bring salvation to the uttermost parts of the earth" (Acts 13:47).

In our discussion, however, we want to concentrate on the church which, like the Servant, also undergoes suffering. Jesus repeatedly instructed his disciples to be prepared for the ministry of suffering: "They will deliver you up to councils, and flog you in their synagogues. . . . When they persecute you. . ." (Mt. 10:17, 23). He spoke to them about bearing the cross in following him (16:24). In the upper room discourse Jesus

warned his disciples about being hated and persecuted, and that persecutors would be under deception of doing God's service in killing them (Jn.
15:18, 20; 16:2). According to these teachings of
Jesus the suffering and affliction of the disciples
were but an extension of his own suffering and humiliation.

Since the suffering of Christ was interpreted as
a fulfillment of the Servant who suffered vicariously for the sake of others, we ought not to be surprised to read that his disciples as servants of God
also endured suffering vicariously. Paul indeed
wrote that his sufferings were the completion of
the afflictions of Christ for the sake of the church:
"Now I rejoice in my sufferings for your sake, and
in my flesh I complete what is lacking in Christ's
afflictions for the sake of his body, that is, the
church" (Col. 1:24). To complete what was lacking in the afflictions of Christ, according to the
Apostle, would not militate against Christ being
preeminent and having the fullness of God (1:18-
19) ; nor did this detract from Christ's reconciling
all things to God (1:20-22). The suffering of
Christ found its continuance in the members of the
church, his body, who should bear afflictions vicariously for the sake of the church.

In II Corinthians the Apostle declared that to
the degree that he and Timothy shared abundantly
in the suffering of Christ they abundantly experienced the comfort of Christ, which is to say that
they realized special strength which they would not
have known without suffering. However, the participation in the sufferings of Christ was not pri-

marily for receiving comfort, but for giving comfort and salvation to the members of the church: "If we are afflicted, it is for your comfort and salvation; and if we are comforted, it is for your comfort, which you experience when you patiently endure the same sufferings that we suffer" (II Cor. 1:6). The Apostle conceived his suffering to be a means of bringing comfort and salvation. It would be comfort and strength for the church in her affliction, for she could then recall the Apostle's steadfastness and joy in his affliction and these would also be her comfort through Christ. And it would be salvation, since the church would be kept from despair and bitterness, if not apostasy, because of affliction. Paul further declared that the sustaining comfort in the midst of all afflictions was an evidence of the transcending power of God (4:7-10).

John, in his first epistle, taught that love required a demonstration of the giving of life for the brethren: "By this we know love, that he laid down his life for us; and we ought to lay down our lives for the brethren" (3:16). The sacrifice of Christ does not require our sacrificial giving to him, but for the brethren. Love, therefore, should extend itself to undergo suffering for the church.

The vicarious suffering of Christ retains its unique purpose of being the reconciliation of the world, both Jew and Gentile, to God (Eph. 2:16), and indeed the reconciliation of all things on earth and in heaven to God (Col. 1:20). The suffering which the Christian bears can be vicarious for members in the church in that by patiently bear-

215

ing affliction he can show the sustaining power of God to others who, in their times of affliction, may know that that comfort can be theirs as well. Suffering thus becomes a ministry which can produce in others patience, steadfastness, and positive attitudes toward life whenever burdens or discouragements occur.

The problem of the suffering, disgrace, and persecution of the righteous will ever perplex the saints who trust in an all-loving, truly just, and omnipotent God. The inequities which the godly encounter seem to mock a faith in a God like that. Many, in their bewilderment and confusion, in loud laments or in quiet musings, have searched the earth and heavens for answers. In the Bible, even as Job learned, the problem still remains an incomprehensible mystery, yet rays of light shine through the darkness to bring some relief to the ones afflicted.[4]

We have observed (1) that affliction brings a correction for life and a new understanding which are not learned in times of prosperity and success. (2) In affliction the godly one can demonstrate that his piety is genuine, that he had indeed achieved spiritual maturity which can exist without rewards. Also (3) times of stress and strain are designed to promote patient faithfulness in living, for at the right time God will vindicate the right and destroy the wrong. Further (4) in suffering the saint realizes fellowship with God that no longer requires vindication or answers for the questionings of heart, for God is present in mercy and grace in every distress. And finally (5) the righteous may suffer vicariously for the comfort and salvation of others. Here we reach the pinnacle of any understanding of the problem, for it is at this point that we see the rich meaning of the sufferings of Christ for the salvation of the world.

NOTES

1. My reasons for this translation instead of "therefore I despise myself" are given in "The Repentance of Job," *The Reformed Review*, Vol. 9 (June, 1956), pp. 40-41; *Vetus Testamentum*, Vol. 9 (1959), pp. 91-95.

2. The literature on the Servant of the LORD is immense. A few recent significant works are noted: C. R. North, *The Suffering Servant in Deutero-Isaiah* (London: Oxford University Press, 1956). This is a most thorough work with an extensive bibliography. A summary appears in "The Servant of the Lord," *The Interpreter's Dictionary of the Bible*, R-Z (Nashville: Abingdon Press, 1962), pp. 292-94. H. H. Rowley, *The Servant of the Lord and Other Essays on the Old Testament* (London: Lutterworth Press, 1952), pp. 3-57; O. Eissfeldt, "The Ebed-Jahwe in Isaiah xl.-lv. in the Light of the Israelite Conceptions of the Community and the Individual, the Ideal and the Real," *The Expository Times*, XLIV (1932-33), pp. 261-68; H. W. Robinson, *The Cross in the Old Testament* (Philadelphia: The Westminster Press, 1955), pp. 65-80.

3. A concise survey is given by J. Jeremias, "The Servant of God in the New Testament," *The Servant of God*. Studies in Biblical Theology 20 (Naperville, Ill.: Alec R. Allenson, Inc., 1957), pp. 79-104.

4. Additional bibliography: A. S. Peake, *The Problem of Suffering in the Old Testament* (London: The Ep-

worth Press, 1904) ; O. A. Piper, "Suffering and Evil," *The Interpreter's Dictionary of the Bible*, R-Z (1962), pp. 450-53; H. W. Robinson, *Suffering Human and Divine* (London: SCM Press, 1940) ; E. F. Sutcliffe, *Providence and Suffering in the Old and New Testaments* (New York: Thomas Nelson and Sons, 1953).

CHAPTER VIII

THE SUFFERING AND REPENTANCE OF GOD

MUCH RESEARCH IN BIBLICAL STUDIES TODAY concerns itself with hermeneutics, that is, principles of interpretation which will do justice to the meaning of the Bible. The need for hermeneutics for the understanding of any literature and especially of the Scripture is apparent since an understanding of the Bible involves the subjective element of the interpreter's faith. In contrast to much literature the Bible asks the reader for his interest, his faith, and his commitment to God. Consequently, subjective notions and arbitrary fancies frequently play a part in determining what the interpretation should be. Before the reader has been properly disciplined in understanding the language of other peoples living in ancient times, he has set up rules of interpretation which satisfy his own predilections but hardly the message of the inspired writer.

Hermeneutics finds its greatest challenge in working with anthropomorphisms, the descriptions of God in terms of human forms and feelings (anthropopathisms). The anthropomorphism attempts to explain the unknown in terms of the known, in this case describing God in terms of our daily experience. The expression "the eyes of God," therefore, tells us that God sees, and in seeing is aware of the world of action and movement. Similarly, ascribing other bodily parts such as mouth, face, hand, or finger to God portrays him as a person who observes people and actually lives in fellowship with them. Much like the parables of Jesus these anthropomorphisms picture the God-man relationship in terms of our common life.

The anthropomorphism, however, valuable as it may be for purposes of communication, poses limitations in our understanding of God. The Old Testament itself would certainly be the first to admit the limitation of anthropomorphism, or any type of language for that matter, for defining the LORD God of Israel. Observe questions such as: "To whom then will you liken God, or what likeness compare with him?" or, "To whom then will you compare me, that I should be like him? says the Holy One" (Is. 40:18, 25). In a discerning article on the topic, *"Die Grenzen des Anthropomorphismus Jahwes im Alten Testament,"*[1] J. Hempel points up the limitations in the use of justice to describe God, for the justice of God has qualities unlike anything found in the justice of men. God's justice does not come within the scope of man's laws and courts, yet it is true that man's justice is or should be a reflection of God's justice. In the sphere of life also we sense the folly of confining God to life as we know it. To be sure, God is alive, even as we are alive; our life in some measure resembles the life of God who created us. Yet God's life cannot be restricted to life as we have it. Sex life, which Israel's neighbors freely ascribed to their gods, was in no instance incorporated within the being of the God of Israel. This kind of popular anthropomorphism so commonly employed by the people of Canaan regarding their gods was most abhorrent to writers of the Old Testament. Yet these same writers would apply the descriptive words "father" and "husband" to the LORD. Consequently, the anthropomorphisms of fatherhood and marriage pose some limitations in the understanding of God. Hempel's list of justice, life, and sexuality can be expanded to take in other anthropomorphisms which would show that each representation of God under some human likeness carries with it some limitation in the understanding of God.

The language limitation sets a task of momentous consequence before the interpreter of the Bible. Two obvious perils beset him: to *under*-interpret, or to *over*-interpret. In the first case he would deny God any "humaneness"; and in the second case he would reduce God to human frailty and absurdity. No doubt every student of the Bible strives to avoid either extreme. Consequently he establishes for himself his own set of rules. These often are embodied in creedal formulations; more often they develop subtly and unwittingly so that the interpreter is hardly aware how his principles of interpretation took shape. And having taken shape they become presuppositions as self-evident and incontestable as axioms in geometry.

H. M. Kuitert, in a well-documented study on the church's problem with anthropomorphisms,

221

points out that principles of interpretation used by the early church became classic solutions for later struggles with anthropomorphisms.[2] The early interpreters came out of Platonic philosophy with its concepts of a transcendent God beyond human comprehension. Since in several instances the Bible also speaks about God's transcendence, natural (hellenic) theology was easily identified with biblical theology to the degree that the former became the norm for determining the teaching of the Bible. Thus in their exposition of Scripture the early church fathers were controlled by presuppositions based on Platonic theology. Kuitert observes that this control was especially evident as they confronted anthropomorphisms in which the divine Being appears in immanent relationship with man. In such situations they established a distinction, perhaps a tension, between God as he really is and God as he reveals himself.[3] Transcendence would be God in reality; anthropomorphism would not be God in reality, but God in revelation. The anthropomorphism is an accommodation device to bring God within man's comprehension. The properly enlightened interpreter would therefore detect within the Scripture the accommodation or adaptation passages which have no significance for understanding God as he actually is. The accommodation principle became the prevailing means for keeping the data of the Bible within the framework of a preconceived theology.

The Suffering of God

The well-known controversy about the suffering of God, known as patripassianism, graphically displays the difficulty of compressing the data of the Bible into the mold of established presuppositions. In his survey of the doctrine on impassibility J. K. Mozley rightly observes that both the Old Testament and the New Testament were not sensitive to the metaphysical interests prevailing in Greek theology.[4] In spite of their declarations about "the high and lofty One who inhabits eternity" (Is. 57:15), the writers of the Bible unreservedly place God within the sphere of human experience so that the prophet also declares that "in all their affliction he was afflicted" (Is. 63:9). Since the church fathers of both the early and medieval church were committed to the doctrine of God's impassibility, they were obliged to bring the biblical statements about God's passibility into line with the orthodox view of impassibility. The solution for the difficulty was sought in defining the two natures of Christ. All suffering, grief, and sorrow were experienced in the human nature of Christ, whereas the divine nature did not participate in human suffering. Patripassianism, which ascribed suffering to God the Father, was condemned as heresy. The impassibility of God was therefore maintained by the fathers' careful defining of the human and divine natures of Christ.

Mozley's book has evoked further study by biblical scholars on the suffering of God.[5] Scholars of recent times have become increasingly dissatisfied with claims for biblical support of impassibility. The opinion, one could possibly say conviction, that the church, even the post-reformation church, has been reading the Bible through the lens of Platonic or Aristotelian theology has gained credence. Nothing calls this reading, or misreading, of the Scripture into question more than a proper understanding of anthropomorphisms in general, and a coming to grips with the passibility of God in particular. This is not to say that exegetical studies of previous ages have become passe; rather it is to allow our present insights to correct or modify the accepted results of former insights. All this, it is hoped, will bring about a truly vital understanding of the Bible.[6]

The above discussion on the interpretation of anthropomorphisms intends to set a background against which we may project the interpretation of the repentance of God. What we have learned about the church's presuppositions based on hellenic theology will help us to understand the principles of exegesis that predetermined the interpretation of passages that deal with God's repentance. Mozley, particularly in his work on the history of impassibility, and Kuitert, in his recent work on the human descriptions of God, are challenging biblical scholars to let the Scripture make its witness unencumbered by scholarly and philosophical preconceptions, however well-intentioned they may be. In the conclusion to his book Mozley raises six necessary questions which should be discussed and answered "with some degree of adequacy, before the problem of suffering in God can

224

be at all satisfactorily dealt with."[7] Four of these six questions will serve us well as points of inquiry to help us arrive at an adequate understanding of the immutability and the mutability of God. The four questions are the following:

1. What is meant by the name God? If God and the Absolute are one, then what are the consequences of predicating finitude about him? Do assertions of passibility or impassibility have any value for understanding God who is the Absolute?

2. What is the true doctrine of God's relationship to the world, especially to creation? What meaning does God's transcendence have for his immanence, and his immanence for his transcendence?

3. Can the life of God be essentially blessed and happy, if it is an eternal life which cannot be influenced in any way by time, in which suffering occurs? Does God's condescension into time affect his essential blessedness?

4. Is a real religious value secured by the idea of the passibility of God? Mozley presses the question further to ascertain whether the suffering of God occurs because of the world, in which case the nature of God is under a constraint which the world places upon it; or whether God suffers because he freely associates himself with the suffering of mankind because of his love and compassion. Is religious value enhanced by God's freely taking to himself the suffering of the world because of his graciousness?

The Repentance and the Non-Repentance of God

The controversy about the impassibility of God frequently involved discussing the immutability of God. Defenders of impassibility appealed to God's unchangeableness to support their point of view. However, the doctrine of immutability never took on the significance of a controversy. One is hard pressed to explain the different levels of interest in discussing these two descriptions of the divine Being. Perhaps the Christological controversies and the debates on the doctrine of the atonement made the doctrine concerning the suffering of God a livelier issue. Whatever the reason, the question of God's immutability receives little attention, and that primarily when preachers or expositors encounter passages that make declarations about God's repentance.[8]

A review of the interpretation of God's repentance will help us sense the problem as the church has seen it and will establish a background against which we may discuss the immutability or mutability of God. Even though this review will be brief, it will present the explanations at which biblical scholars have arrived in their struggles with passages that declare that God repents.

History of Interpretation

In his essay, "On the Unchangeableness of God," Philo interprets the passages of Genesis 6:6-7 which speak about God's repentance.[9] Even though Philo uses for his discussion the LXX

Greek, which softens the idea of God's repenting to his having the matter in mind and being angry, he is fully aware of the Hebrew's use of the word "repenting" and declares that it is a great impiety to speak of the Creator as repenting. Such impiety is greater than the wickedness about which the chapter deals. If there is constancy among the best on earth, how would anyone dare to think of God in terms of changeability? Since the Creator is above the change and growth within the creation, he cannot be regarded as subject to change. In the first instance where the Hebrew verb is used the LXX suggests that God had it in his mind that he had made man, which is interpreted to mean that God considered that he had made man a rational free being, and that it was the misuse of freedom which produced the wickedness in the earth. The second occurrence of the verb is rendered to mean that God was angry that he had made man. This causes Philo difficulty since God is not subject to human passions such as wrath or anger. His exegesis, which suffers from lack of clarity, suggests that Moses the Lawgiver speaks about God's anger to frighten the foolish into proper reverence for God. In other words, anger is not a proper quality to be found in God, but only a device to show man how wicked he has become and to move him from sin to seek the grace of God, as Noah did. Philo therefore dismisses the Hebrew sense of repentance and the Greek translation of anger as concepts not to be found in God, although he freely ascribes the equally human trait of thinking and reflecting to him.[10]

Augustine, in his comments on passages in which repentance of God occurs, states that all things are arranged and fixed by God from the beginning. In the change which occurs in temporal things there is no change in the matters which were decreed by the immutability of God's most secret will. God has already done both the present and the future things. Here the church father muses on the wonder of the comprehensive and immutable will. When it is said that God "repented according to the greatness of his mercy" he did what he had arranged to do beforehand. God foreknew that his people would pray to him out of their tribulation and, because of this prayer which he foreknew, he would change their captivity into deliverance (Ps. 106:45).[11] In his comment on Psalm 132:11 Augustine observes that when God is said to change he changes his words or deeds, but he does not change his immutable will.

Jerome, a contemporary of Augustine, in his commentary on Jeremiah 18:1-10 relates the repentance of God to the exercise of Israel's freedom of choice. If Israel turns from evil to uprightness then God will hold back the threatened evil; and if Israel forsakes uprightness to turn to evil, then the promised good will not come upon the people. Freedom of decision must be maintained.[12] Jerome has some qualms about the propriety of using the word "perhaps" *(forsitan)* in Jeremiah 26:3, "perhaps they will listen, and every one turn from his evil way, that I may repent of the evil which I intend to do to them." Surely God knows all future things, consequently it seems improper to ascribe uncertainty to God. Jerome, however, approves this contingency on the part of God as necessary for our benefit. In fact, Jerome finds the "perhaps" in the Evangel: "I will send my son, perhaps they will honor him" (Lk. 20:13). The repentance of God, therefore, has no bearing on God, who is above change and uncertainty, but does have bearing on man, who must exercise his choice of freedom.

Cornelius A. Lapide in his comments on Genesis 6:6-7[13] observes that it is improper to speak of God's repenting or grieving. The repenting here, however, must be understood to mean that because of the hardness of men God retracts his gifts and casts out the sinner whom he has created. According to Lapide the Vulgate rendering of Joel 2:13, *Et praestabilis super malitia,* "And he is established above evil," has a more elegant meaning than the Hebrew text, "And he repents concerning evil," for the Vulgate passage declares that God stands above all evil such as wrath or vengeance, and does not allow himself to be conquered by evil, but as LORD rules over it. The Vulgate of Jonah 3:10, "God was compassionate over their evil," means that God's compassion should move godly people to treat repentant sinners with compassion. Lapide's comment on Jonah 4:2 states that the threatening oracles of God are conditional, even though this is not stated explicitly. Consequently there is no change in God, but only in the accused sinners. Since God is immutable, most wise, and aware of and foreknowing all future things, neither grief nor penitence can fall on him.

In his repentance God withdraws his promised blessings because of man's ingratitude and unworthiness, as in the case of King Saul (I Sam. 15:11).

Although John Calvin's comments on the repentance of God differ little from the prevailing exegesis prior to the Reformation, yet our study will profit from a survey of Calvin's thought on passages we have already discussed. Regarding Genesis 6:6-7, Calvin declares that repentance cannot properly be ascribed to God, for nothing unforseen or unexpected can happen to God. And the same reasoning would keep us from attributing grief to God, for certainly, says Calvin, nothing sorrowful or sad can happen to God who forever remains himself in his celestial happiness and repose. These words of repentance and grief are to be understood to point to God's severe detestation of sin, and to point out to man his extreme wickedness.[14]

Discussing Moses' intercession for Israel, Exodus 32:12-14, Calvin manifests some uneasiness about God's not consummating the threatened destruction which in his wrath he said he would bring upon the apostate people. Surely God's word must come to pass. If this is a problem, and in truth it is a problem for Calvin, then his solution is offered in two not closely related suggestions: (1) We here confront an incomprehensible mystery which God is not obliged to explain to us; and (2) we are here instructed about God as judge, his doom upon sin, and his pardon which was being withheld. Calvin further adds in his comment for this passage that God's repentance is a change in dealing with Israel, which is tantamount to his being appeased.

In other passages that deal with the repentance of God Calvin affirms that no change takes place in God, but that rather a change takes place in man. Man becomes aware of his desperate plight and of the punishment which the wrath of God will bring upon him. Consequently, man turns away from his sin to experience the pardoning grace of God.

Since Calvin sets the repentance of God in the realm of mystery, he must deal with the limitations of language in describing something about God which is beyond our grasp. In fact, it appears that the anthropopathetic repentance is misleading, because it suggests the concept of mutability in God, instead of the intended concept of pardon which mitigates or withholds the pronounced punishment. Calvin asserts that the threatened doom is conditional even when conditions are not expressed. Because of these implied conditional factors in all threats, it becomes possible for God to repent of sending the threatened destruction because certain conditions were fulfilled that allowed him to refrain from the evil and to pardon the sin.[15]

In his controversy with Socinus on the immutability of God, F. Turretin demonstrates rationally that complete immutability must be ascribed to God as follows: God is able to change neither for the better since he is the best, nor for the worse since he is defined as the most perfect. Therefore, all reasons for change, such as dependence on prior things, permissive power, error of mind, and inconstancy of will do not affect God. When penitence is ascribed to God as in Genesis 6:6-8, this must not be understood as *pathêtikos,* a suffering or distress, but as *euergetikos,* a showing of kindness or beneficence. When it is ascribed to God penitence must be understood as *theoprepôs,* that is, befitting God, which means that it occurs not because of deliberation but because of the event, not of the will itself, but of the thing willed, not of the state of mind and internal grief, but of accomplishment and external work because he does what penitent man is accustomed to do.[16]

The definitive work of Protestant scholasticism on the immutability of God was produced by Stephen Charnocke in his *Discourses upon the Existence and Attributes of God.*[17] This elaborate exposition moves from proper exegesis of Scripture to interpretations controlled by presuppositions. Here one readily observes the tension, as expressed by Kuitert, between God as he really is and God as he reveals himself. The God of reality possesses perfection of blessedness and joy, and immutability of will and purpose from eternity. At those places in Scripture where God's immutability or perfection is brought into question, one encounters the God of revelation, that is, the God of reality accommodating himself to human understanding. Charnocke asserts that repentance and other affections ascribed to God are not evidence of change in God. Since God is pure Spirit he is not capable of passions which show weakness and impotence. Repentance and grief are unworthy descriptions of

God, for they are inconsistent with his undefiled blessedness. Though Scripture ascribes parts of the body to God, we should not conclude that he has a body like ours; similarly we should not conclude from ascriptions of repentance and grief that he has human passions. These descriptions are the language of accommodation which do not in reality describe the God of reality. Ascribing repentance to God describes change in his outward conduct without any change in his immutable will. The use of repentance and grief to describe him intends to represent his detestation for sin and to move man to repentance and grief.

Should one pursue a study of theologians such as Charles Hodge, William G. T. Shedd, A. H. Strong, or L. Berkhof, to mention a few, he would find restatements of the work of F. Turretin and S. Charnocke on the problem of God's repentance. The data of the Bible are divided into two levels: the upper level which embraces the teachings about God's transcendence and immutability and is given unqualified credence and acceptance, for this level describes the God of reality; and the lower level with its teachings about God's immanence and repentance, which does not enjoy unqualified credence and acceptance but is subjected to arbitrary interpretation to relieve the tension arising between these two levels. The latter level is described in the language of accommodation, which by definition does not describe God as he is in himself.

The preceding survey of the work of Protestant scholars reveals a labored effort to avoid the obvious meaning of passages which speak about

God's repentance. In its exegesis on the being of God Protestantism has largely followed the patterns and presuppositions of medieval scholasticism which, as Brunner has pointed out, were based on speculations of Platonism and Neo-Platonism.[18] This legacy of Greek thought persisted into post-Reformation exegesis with the result that Protestant scholars were inclined to balk at any suggestion of change in God. Consequently they were obliged to resort to a devious exegesis to avoid the obvious statement that there might be a change in God's manner of dealing with his people.

One of the first to give some recognition to God's changeability as expressed in Scripture was J. A. Dorner in his essay on "The Proper Comprehension of the Dogmatic Concept of the Unchangeableness of God."[19] Dorner observes that there exists a theological tension between the unchangeableness and transcendence of God on the one hand, and his vitality and immanence on the other hand. The author asks in what kind of being unchangeableness and vitality might exist, and defines it as the ethical being of God which expresses itself in freedom and love. This ethical being is what may be called the unchangeableness of God who in his ethical purpose expresses himself in freedom and love. This kind of vitality expresses itself so strongly that one can observe, on the one hand, a rigid unchangeableness in God and, on the other hand, a flexibility in God's act which establishes man's freedom in the influence which qualifies the divine act.

We conclude this survey of interpretation with

a brief note on Karl Barth's discussion of "The Constancy and Omnipotence of God," to which I refer with special appreciation.[20] In his review of the scholastic treatment of the immutability of God Barth notes that scholasticism has not found the God of the Bible. The immutable God of the Bible is the One who is forever acting in freedom and love. In fact, the constancy of God is to be demonstrated and seen in his freedom and love, which he never surrenders but always at every point manifests vividly. This is far from the pagan notion of the immobile God, a notion, says Barth, which is only a euphemistic description of death. If we may accept the immutability of God as primarily manifested in his freedom and love, then we may have some direction by which to understand and to discuss the repentance and non-repentance of God.

Questions on God's Repentance

We shall now take up four of the six questions Mozley proposed for his particular discussion about the suffering of God. It will be necessary to recast the questions to relate them to our discussion of the repentance of God.

1. What is meant by the concept God? If God and the Absolute are the same, then what are the consequences of predicating changeability and unchangeability about him?

The concept of God must take into account declarations about both his unchangeability and his changeability. Let one citation for each suffice to establish the point. "And also the Glory of Israel will not lie or repent; for he is not a man, that he should repent" (I Sam. 15:29); "And the LORD repented that he had made Saul king over Israel" (I Sam. 15:35). This chapter deals with the rejection of Saul in which God both repents of his previous choice and will not repent of his decision to reject Saul as king.

This chapter and other such citations offer two views about God that speak meaningfully for Christian faith and life. In the first instance the unchangeability of God assures us that we are not at the mercy of caprice or irresponsible power which often characterizes the conduct of man. This unchangeability is preeminently reflected in the LORD's covenantal faithfulness to Israel. In the second instance, the changeability of God manifests God in vital relationship with his people. Israel was not in the hands of an iron fate or a predetermined order. Rather, the opposite was true, for the LORD took into account all aspects of Israel's life, whether it was their waywardness, oppression by enemies, or penitence. Consequently, Israel knew that her manner of life had direct bearing on God's rule over Israel.

The term Absolute suggests concepts and images of tyrannical power and of exalted detachment from mankind and the world. If God in his absoluteness is conceived of as existing in isolation and in no way affected by the experiences of mankind, then the title Absolute should be banned from our Christian vocabulary. Appeals to the biblical witness of the immutability of God to support the title Absolute must be countered by recognition of the abundant testimony to his changeability.

The Holy One, as a convenient synonym for the Absolute, is usually defined as God exalted and separated from man, sin, and the world (Is. 6:1-8). The Holy One dwells in the high and holy place and inhabits eternity (Is. 57:15); and he is beyond any comparison with man and creation (Is. 40:25). However, to restrict the meaning of Holy One to the wholly Other is to ignore declarations of the prophet about the Holy One's being the Creator of Israel (43:1, 15) and the Savior and Redeemer of Israel (43:3, 14; 47:4; 49:26). Furthermore, the Holy One dwells in the midst of his people (57:15; Hos. 11:9). The concept of Holy One, much like that of Absolute, derives from a limited use of Scripture.

To conclude, we may assert that predicating changeability and unchangeability about God is, on the one hand, to take all Scripture into account, and, on the other hand, to embrace a balanced concept of God which has assurance and meaning for life.

2. What is the proper doctrine of God's relationship to the world, especially to creation? What meaning does God's immutability have for his mutability, and his mutability for his immutability?

The Old Testament declares that "in six days the LORD made heaven and earth, the sea, and all that is in them" (Ex. 20:11). The LORD, in freedom and in sovereign power, created the world and declared that "it was very good" (Gen. 1:31). The battle of the gods in pagan myths of creation has no place in the Old Testament; neither is God caught up in the cycle of the natural order. Creation is not the result of a struggle in which God emerges victorious; neither is God to be identified with the productive powers of nature as was done in Canaanite religion. Rather, in freedom God both establishes and employs creation in his covenantal relationship with Israel. This means, on the one hand, that according to the covenant made with Noah the order of creation is firmly established to serve mankind, and, on the other hand, that according to the covenant made in the land of Moab (Deut. 28) God's use of the forces of nature is contingent upon Israel's obedience or disobedience.

To view the LORD's relationship to creation and the natural order properly one must see it in the setting of his acts in Israel's history. God's rule in nature plays a functional role in his control over Israel's life and destiny. The east wind blows to make a dry passage through the Sea for Israel's escape; the waters of Megiddo become a torrent to deliver Israel from the army of Canaan. Furthermore, nature can become punitive in that the plague, the drought, or the locust brings the LORD's judgment upon Israel. Creation, then, is not an entity by itself to awaken awe and wonder in the heart of the worshipper, but rather the instrument through which God acts in the life and destiny of Israel.

In what way does God's relationship to and use of nature have bearing on his immutability and his mutability? In the fixed order of creation as described in the covenant with Noah and elsewhere we sense the immutable dependability of God. Despite the destructive judgment of the flood God preserves the order of creation and declares that it shall continue even as it was designed in the beginning. Neither man's sin nor the resurgence of the watery chaos can destroy the order of God's creation. The established permanence of creation reflects the unchangeability of its Creator. The unchangeableness of the natural order as described in the Old Testament serves as counterpart to the immutability of God.

However, the powers of nature display wide variation in their effects on man. In some instances fields and flocks enjoy abundant increase to delight man in his labors; but in other instances blight and disease, or drought and locust cause the land to mourn and bring heaviness and dismay to man. Why is creation so erratic, lavishing its abundance at times and withholding its bountiful store at other times? The Old Testament writers attribute these varying phenomena to the immediate direction of God who takes into account the obedience and the disobedience of Israel. Here the variability of the natural order reflects the changeability of God's rule over Israel. Deuteronomy tells us that

> if you obey the voice of the LORD your God
> . . . the LORD will make you abound in pros-
> perity, in the fruit of your body, and in the fruit
> of your cattle, and in the fruit of your
> ground. . . . But if you will not obey the
> voice of the LORD your God to be careful to do

239

> all his commandments and his statutes which I command you this day, then all these curses shall come upon you and overtake you. . . . Cursed shall be the fruit of your body, and the fruit of your ground, the increase of your cattle, and the young of your flock (28:1, 11, 15, 18).

One observes, therefore, that the data of the Old Testament which have bearing on the immutability and the mutability of God point to a relationship between God, nature, and Israel which illustrates the nature of God's unchangeability and changeability. Some may call this a contradiction, others a paradox, and still others contrapletal logic.[21] Whatever we may choose to name these two concepts, the appearance of both is clearly evident in the Old Testament, and recognizing them gives us a profound description of God's vital relationship with his people Israel.

3. Can the life of God be essentially blessed and happy if grief, regret, or repentance takes place within it? Does God's participation in the events of Israel's life, with its amalgam of happy fruition and dismaying futility, affect his essential blessedness?

In discussing the impassibility of God, as Mozley points out, scholars have been wont to regard pain as part of the human experience which man encounters because of his sin and from which man will be freed when he enjoys the blessedness of heaven. Since suffering could not be associated with blessedness the conclusion seemed self-evident that God's blessedness must be free from all suffering. Mozley raises the question whether the life of God can be essentially blessed and happy as he enters time, in which suffering takes place. B. R. Brasnett examines this question to conclude that the necessity of God's being impassible to have pure blessedness rests on our definition of blessedness. From our point of view we determine what pure blessedness should be. This kind of procedure indulges a begging of the question that halts any further inquiry. Further, Brasnett explores Mozley's diffident inquiry whether the Incarnation and its suffering is simply a revealing episode in the Life of God the Son. Brasnett rejects the idea, implied in the inquiry, that this revealing episode within history has no bearing on the essential Being of God. Brasnett underlines Kuitert's caveat, noted above, against positing God as he really is in contrast to God as he reveals himself.[22]

Sorrow, regret, and repentance are readily identified with suffering so that scholars in the history of interpretation find them incompatible with the blessedness of God. Calvin speaks about God who is not sorrowful or sad but remains forever the same in his celestial and happy repose. Charnocke observes that God who is blessed forever (Rom. 9:5) can have nothing befall him to impair that blessedness, something which repentance and grief would seem to do.[23] Much like the defenders of impassibility, interpreters have sought to protect the blessedness of God against any biblical statements of regret or repentance that would mar the essential happiness of God.

241

Such well-meaning concern about God's blessedness, however, leads to a faulty interpretation in at least two respects. The first has to do with the understanding and defining of blessedness. To assert that the repentance of God is incompatible with his blessedness is an arbitrary statement that predetermines the conclusion being sought. Apparently the writers of Scripture, who were certainly as concerned with the honor and dignity of God as any interpreter might be, sensed no incompatibility between God's repentance and his exalted blessedness. It seems plausible that the blessedness of God would include a variety of emotional life including regret, grief, and repentance.

The second respect involves the issue of integrity in the use and the interpretation of the biblical witness. Concern for God's blessedness hardly justifies irresponsible and capricious handling of Scripture, which clearly declares that God is unchangeable and does not repent: "God is not man, that he should lie, or a son of man, that he should repent" (Num. 23:19) ; "The Glory of Israel will not lie or repent; for he is not a man, that he should repent" (I Sam. 15:29) ; "Every perfect gift is from above, coming down from the Father of lights with whom there is no variation or shadow due to change" (Jas. 1:17) .[24] But with equal clarity Scripture affirms that God is changeable and does repent: "And the LORD repented of the evil which he thought to do to his people" (Ex. 32:14) ; "Nevertheless he regarded their distress, when he heard their cry. He remembered for their sake his covenant, and repented according to the abundance of his steadfast love" (Ps. 106:44-45); "When God saw what they did, how they turned from their evil way, God repented of the evil which he had said he would do to them; and he did not do it" (Jon. 3:10).[25]

One may venture the surmise that the essential blessedness of God is less disturbed by a forthright acceptance of passages on changeability and repentance, than by a crafty exegesis of such passages.

4. What is the religious significance of the repentance of God? Or more fully, what is the religious value of both the non-repentance and the repentance of God? Does God's unqualified unchangeableness leave open the possibility for a meaningful divine-human relationship? Or does it reduce mankind's struggle to a hollow mockery, full of sound and fury, meaning nothing?

In formulating his question on the passibility of God Mozley raises the significant inquiry whether "God is thought of as suffering because the world leaves Him no option . . . or whether God is said to suffer because in His love He freely associates with the world's suffering by means of a true compassion."[26] To rephrase the above inquiry, we ask whether God's repentance takes place because the course of the world's events leaves no other course for him to take, or whether God freely changes his course of action to demonstrate a genuine association with his people.

Let us first ascertain the religious significance

243

of God's non-repentance. The Apostle Paul, in his concern for Israel, observes that God has lavished gifts such as sonship, glory, covenants, law, worship, and promises on his people (Rom. 9:4-5), so that they are beloved of God for the sake of their forefathers (11:28). The basis for Israel's being beloved is expressed in Paul's summary declaration that the charismatic gifts and the call of God are not to be repented of, *ametameleta* (11:29). This remarkable statement appears like a maxim which, because of its common acceptance, needs no proof. In fact, in this succinct form it serves as a distillation of God's gracious relationship with Israel. Any study of the Old Testament cannot but agree that God never repented of his call of Israel nor of his many gifts to them. Here we may properly speak of the unchangeability of God, as far as it relates to the bestowal of his gifts upon his people.

The religious value inherent in God's immutability, therefore, is not to be found in a predestined order of events but rather in the ever-flowing stream of charismatic favors on the people called by God to enrich the life of the world. The unchangeableness of God is not properly understood in terms of transcendent detachment from his people, but is rather to be associated with beneficent generosity which St. James aptly defines in his epistle: "Every good endowment and every perfect gift is from above, coming down from the Father of lights with whom there is no variation or shadow due to change" (1:16).

What is the religious significance of the repentance of God? A survey of Old Testament witness

244

on this subject makes plain that the repentance of God always takes place in the God-Israel relationship and makes that relationship meaningful. Furthermore in this divine-human encounter God responds to man's action within an ethical setting. Man's conduct is taken into account to make God's moral integrity clear and to demonstrate that God deals with man as a responsible moral being. And finally, the repentance of God expresses itself frequently in compassion and mercy.

We read of the repentance of God which takes place in response to the intercessory prayer of the prophet. In the golden calf incident at Sinai (Ex. 32:1-14) the LORD, in his wrath, determines to destroy Israel for their waywardness in worshipping the image. Moses intercedes for Israel and beseeches the LORD to turn from his fierce anger and to repent of the evil planned for the people. Because of this intercession the LORD repents of the evil he planned to do. Similarly, Amos intercedes for Israel in his prayer, "How can Jacob stand? He is so small!" (7:2, 5). And the LORD repents of his pronounced judgment. The changeability of God in response to the prayer of man indicates that man participates in a meaningful relationship with God. Man at prayer is not a puppet whose words are set on tape to be spoken at the proper time. Rather, God takes into account the pleas of his prophets.

Jeremiah sets the repentance of God in the context of his oracles of doom. However, the declared doom will be averted if Israel turns from evil to good, for then the LORD will repent of the evil planned for his people. Also, a people may be deprived of the promised good if they turn from righteousness to evil, for then the LORD will repent of the good he promised his people (18:7-10). The LORD also took into account the conduct of Nineveh which repented at the preaching of Jonah, for "God repented of the evil which he had said he would do to them" (Jon. 3:10). These are instances of God's response to man's conduct which evidence the moral integrity of God's relationship with Israel and every nation.

A caution against confining the God-Israel relationship within an ethical context as we have described above needs to be made. If God's repentance is restricted to Israel's obedience or disobedience of the law, then religion becomes a bargain-counter experience that changes a living I-thou relationship into a dull *quid pro quo* formalism. Moreover, such a relationship never reaches fulfillment in Israel's history simply because her prevailing way was disobedience and waywardness. The total witness of the Old Testament will not support a neat ethical structure of reward and retribution commensurate with obedience and disobedience, or faithfulness and unfaithfulness. If this were the structure, Israel's destiny would be doomed because of her persistent departure from the law of God. The problem would then emerge, in view of both Israel's inability and her refusal to obey the demands of the law, how God would preserve his people whom he placed in covenant relationship.

246

At this point God's repentance significantly takes into account Israel's sorry plight of being under the judgment of God from which she cannot remove herself. Judgment, however, is not God's last and final word for his people, for he sees their distress and repents of the evil he sent upon them. He is then moved by compassion and mercy to deliver them. The writer of Judges relates that the LORD raised up judges who saved the people, "for the LORD repented because of their groaning" caused by those who oppressed them (Judg. 2:18). Similarly, the psalmist describes the deliverance of Israel in terms of the LORD's hearing the cry of distress, of his remembering for their sakes his covenant, and of his repenting according to the abundance of his faithful love (Ps. 106:44-45). In the tension, as described by Hosea, between God's wrath and his love for Israel, God's repentings are awakened so that he will not execute the fierceness of his anger to destroy Israel (Hos. 11:8-9). His repentance concerning Israel becomes synonymous with his eternal compassion for his people. This repentance appears in a remarkable sequence recurring frequently in Israel's history: a wayward people, divine judgment, a cry of distress, God's repentance, and Israel's deliverance. The main thrust of this sequence is to reveal the overflowing compassion and mercy of God.[27]

The repenting of God from evil that threatened to destroy his people becomes so much a part of the thought and message of prophet and historian that it enters the confessional credo of two prophets. "Return to the LORD, your God,

247

for he is gracious and merciful, slow to anger and abounding in steadfast love *and repents of evil"* (Joel 2:13). "For I knew that thou art a gracious God and merciful, slow to anger, and abounding in steadfast love, *and repentest of evil"* (Jon. 4:2). The credo as given at Sinai was: "A God merciful and gracious, slow to anger, and abounding in steadfast love and faithfulness" (Ex. 34:6). As the inspired historians and prophets observe that in spite of Israel's frequent apostasy God never sends final destruction upon his people, they declare that God repents of the evil pronounced over his people. This repentance was so much an observable factor in Israel's history that later prophets add "repents of evil" as a significant addendum to the Sinai credo.

Mozley's inquiry posed the question whether God suffers because he is caught in circumstances which leave him no choice, or whether God suffers because he freely enters the experiences of man by means of his merciful compassion. In our study to ascertain the religious values secured in the non-repentance and the repentance of God we observe that the Scriptures clearly show that God acts in freedom and compassion. Barth has said well that the immutable God will always manifest himself in his freedom and his love. The practical benefits for Christian faith and life are set within God's freedom and love. God manifests these qualities to us, and these are the qualities we are to manifest to the world.[28]

NOTES

1. J. Hempel, "*Die Grenzen des Anthropomorphismus Jahwes im Alten Testament*," ZAW (1939), pp. 75-85.

2. H. M. Kuitert, *De Mensvormigheid Gods* (Kampen: J. H. Kok N.V., 1962).

3. *Ibid.*, pp. 235-45.

4. J. K. Mozley, *The Impassibility of God* (Cambridge: University Press, 1926).

5. B. R. Brasnett, *The Suffering of the Impassible God* (London: S.P.C.K., 1928); K. Kitamori, *Theology of the Pain of God* (Richmond: John Knox Press, 1965); articles in theological journals are: K. E. Pollard, *Scottish Journal of Theology* (1955), pp. 353-64; G. Wondra, *The Reformed Review* (December, 1964), pp. 28-35; K. J. Woollcombe, *Scottish Journal of Theology* (1967), pp. 129-48.

6. The Netherlands Reformed Church in her Church Order, Article X, makes a declaration appropriate here:

> In thankful obedience to the Holy Scripture as the source for preaching and the only rule of faith, the entire Church, also in her official gatherings, makes confession of the self-revelation of the Triune God in fellowship with the confession of the fathers and in recognition of her responsibility for the present, pressing forward to the coming of Jesus Christ.

7. Mozley, *op. cit.*, p. 177.

8. A study of the verbal root *NHM* and a history of translations appear in *The Reformed Review* (May, 1965), pp. 3-8.

9. "On the Unchangeableness of God," *Philo*, The Loeb Classical Library, Vol. III (New York: G. P. Putnam's Sons), pp. 3-101.

10. According to Philo anthropomorphism is used as a "crutch for our weakness." Observe his discussion on the impropriety of God binding himself with an oath.

> Why then did it seem well to the prophet and revealer to represent God as binding himself with an oath? It was to convince created man of his weakness and to accompany conviction with help and comfort. We are not able to cherish in our souls continually the thought which sums so worthily the nature of the Cause, that "God is not as man" (Num. 23:19), and thus rise superior to all human conceptions of him. . . . Therefore we invent for him hands and feet, incomings and outgoings, enmities, aversions, estrangements, anger, in fact such parts and passions as can never belong to the Cause. And of such is the oath—a mere crutch for our weakness.

Philo, op. cit., Vol. II, pp. 165-67.

11. J. P. Migne, *Patrologia Latina*, XXXVII, 1416.

12. *Ibid.*, XXIV, 796.

13. C. A. Lapide, *Commentaria in Pentateuchum Mosis* (Lugduni [Lyons]: Fratres de Tournes, 1732), p. 84. Other references are from commentaries *in loco*.

14. Calvin's commentaries *in loco*.

15. *Institutes of the Christian Religion*, Bk. I, Chap. XVII, 13, 14.

16. F. Turretin, *Compendium Theologiae Didactico-Elenchticae* (1731), pp. 65-66.

17. S. Charnocke, *Discourses Upon the Existence and Attributes of God* (Henry G. Bohn, London, 1860), pp. 195-230.

250

18. E. Brunner, *The Christian Doctrine of God,* Vol. I (London: Lutterworth Press, 1949), pp. 266-69.

19. J. A. Dorner, "The Proper Comprehension of the Dogmatic Concept of the Unchangeableness of God," *Gesammelte Schriften* (Berlin: Verlag von Wilhelm Hertz, 1883), pp. 188-377.

20. Karl Barth, *Church Dogmatics,* Vol. II/1 (Edinburgh: T. & T. Clark, 1957), pp. 490-500.

21. K. J. Woollcombe introduced this term to me. *Op. cit.,* p. 142. Just as it seems possible "to hold paradoxically that God is both passible and impassible without any breach of 'contrapletal' logic," so it seems possible to bring the concepts of changeability and unchangeability within contrapletal logic.

22. Brasnett, *op. cit.,* pp. 67-79.

23. Charnocke, *op. cit.,* p. 216.

24. Also Ps. 110:4; Jer. 4:28; 20:16; Ezek. 24:14; Zech. 8:14; Mal. 3:6.

25. Also Gen. 6:6-7; Ex. 32:12; Judg. 2:18; I Sam. 15:11, 24; II Sam. 24:16; I Chron. 21:15; Jer. 18:8, 10; 26:3, 13, 19; 42:10; Amos 7:3, 6; Joel 2:13; Jon. 4:2.

26. Mozley, *op. cit.,* p. 181.

27. Jesus similarly declares that the changeability of God becomes evident in his response to tribulation. "And if the Lord had not shortened the days, no human being would be saved; but for the sake of the elect, whom he chose, he shortened the days" (Mk. 13:20).

28. Professor H. Berkhof of Leiden University has made a significant contribution to this subject in "The (Un)changeability of God" in *Grace upon Grace,* James Cook, ed. (Grand Rapids: Wm. B. Eerdmans Publishing Co., 1975), pp. 21-29.

CHAPTER IX

THE HARDNESS
OF HEART

Introduction

THE SCRIPTURES HAVE SERVED THE BELIEVING
community as a guide for faith and conduct. Long
after the prominent personalities such as Abraham,
Moses, and David of the Old Testament and Jesus,
Paul, and John of the New Testament had lived,
spoken, and written, many people of later times
and of different cultures have embraced these
Scriptures with deep devotion and gratitude.

This devotion to the study of the law and its
interpretation began during the time of exile and
continued under Ezra during the restoration in
Palestine. With intense zeal the monastics at
Qumran ordered their lives according to the law
and interpreted the prophets meaningfully for
their times in which Judaism experienced internal
strife. Also during the first century A.D. the schools
of Hillel and of Shammai flourished, and together
with lesser scholars produced many commentaries
on the Old Testament. These eventually became
the great Talmud, Judaism's magnificent study of
the Scriptures to find in them the way of faith and
life.

What describes Judaism's great interest in the

holy writings can equally be ascribed to the Christian church. The church, although it also regarded the Old Testament as Scripture, found itself interpreting the Old Testament in the light of Jesus Christ, his crucifixion and resurrection. This new reading of the law and prophets provoked intense hostility between Christians and Jews. It will not serve our purpose here to defend the Christian witness, but it will be noteworthy to observe that two great religious bodies, Jews and Christians, honored the same holy book, yet each arrived at different understandings of it. Thus it was that early in the history of the church people with high devotion and integrity read the same books and came to violent disagreements as to their proper interpretation.

At this point I get some comfort, cool though it may be, that the violent disagreements that plagued the church in her history had their inception at the time people began to study and interpret this holy book. Perhaps, in a romantic conception of Christian love and unity, one might imagine that once the church had established its center of faith in Jesus Christ, and that once the church had its own Scriptures which interpreted Jesus Christ to the world, disturbing disagreements would fade away. However, the contrary is true, for in the history of the church one finds sharp disputes about interpretation in matters arising out of the New Testament itself. These controversies did not arise from an indifference to the holy writings of the Christians, but, contrariwise, they arose because of an intense desire to know them fully and

253

interpret them faithfully. What happened in the early centuries of the Chistian church was repeated in the succeeding generations: The book which was to be the church's guide and comfort also became the source for its difference of opinion. So we should realize from the outset of our present search to know the Scriptures, that no matter how diligently we may work at understanding we cannot hope to achieve a popular agreement with the results of our research.

The Hardening of the Heart

As we examine the subject of the hardening of the heart in its biblical setting, we encounter passages and texts which are at variance with each other, much as we found in our study of the Repentance of God. The biblical witness, if one accepts it in its entirety, does not present a bland uniformity on a subject that deals with God's relationship with man in his sinful world, but contains a rich variety of material describing the ongoing God-man encounter in the history of redemption. This indeed is the main message of the Bible. Consequently, the hardening of the heart is not a unique problem in the study of Scripture, yet it is a subject that has been treated rather lightly and cavalierly in the interpretations of many ardent and faithful scholars.

In biblical studies we have learned that the account of the exodus from Egypt has become the base on which our faith is built. Let us examine a few of the prominent passages. First of all, we have the revelation of God's name. Moses asked God what his name was, and God answered Moses, "I AM WHO I AM. . . . Say this to the people of Israel, 'I AM has sent me to you.' . . . this is my name for ever, and thus I am to be remembered throughout all generations" (Ex. 3:14-15). The well-known prologue to the Ten Commandments reads, "I am the Lord your God, who brought you out of the land of Egypt, out of the house of bondage" (20:2). This declaration of deliverance for Israel had as its consummation the promise that Israel would become a covenant people: "if you will obey my voice and keep my covenant, you shall be my own possession among all the peoples; for all the earth is mine, and you shall be to me a kingdom of priests and a holy nation" (19:5-6). Moreover, the Ten Commandments served to guide Israel in her response to God's offer of grace. Further, the statement about God and his relationship to Israel is given in these very significant words, "The LORD, the LORD, a God merciful and gracious, slow to anger, and abounding in steadfast love and faithfulness" (34:6). These and other passages can be regarded as the source, not only for Israel's faith but for the faith of the Christian church as well. Therefore, when we reach into this source for any particular point of understanding we are dealing with the basis of the teachings of the Scriptures.

It is here that we read about Pharaoh and the hardening of his heart. This interesting and important phenomenon is described in three different ways. First, Pharaoh himself hardens his heart:

"But when Pharaoh saw that there was a respite, he hardened his heart, and would not listen to them; as the LORD had said" (Ex. 8:15). The second is that the heart of Pharaoh was hardened: "But Pharaoh's heart was hardened, and he would not listen to them; as the LORD had said" (ver. 19). And finally the LORD himself hardens the heart of Pharaoh: "Then the LORD said to Moses, 'Go in to Pharaoh; for I have hardened his heart and the heart of his servants'" (10:1). So it is that we may observe that Pharaoh himself was active, that something acted upon Pharaoh so that he seemed to be passive, and thirdly, that God himself was the agent to create the hardness of heart in Pharaoh and also in the Egyptians.[1]

Pharaoh and the Egyptians are here seen opposing the LORD's deliverance of Israel from bondage. Describing this stubborn resistance, the narrative suggests that the combined activity of God and of Pharaoh bring about the hardened heart of resistance. This resistance or rebellion against God is described in various ways throughout the Old Testament; figures of speech commonly used include blinded eyes, stopped ears, and stiff necks. The prophet Ezekiel is told that the people of Israel are a house of rebellion, people of a hard forehead and of a stubborn heart. In Isaiah's vision and call to be a prophet to Israel he is told to speak to his people and "Make the heart of this people fat, and their ears heavy, and shut their eyes; lest they see with their eyes, and hear with their ears, and understand with their hearts, and turn and be healed" (6:10). Here the prophet is to be the agent to bring on the unrepentant attitude of the people. In another passage of this same prophet we read again of this complex activity in which God and Israel produce the result of hardness of heart or blindness of eyes:

> Stupefy yourselves and be in a stupor,
> blind yourselves and be blind!
> Be drunk, but not with wine;
> stagger, but not with strong drink!
> For the Lord has poured out upon you
> a spirit of deep sleep,
> and has closed your eyes, the prophets,
> and covered your heads, the seers (29:9-10).

Deuteronomy offers a similar instance in which Israel is under the wrath of God because it has forsaken the covenant made with it during the exodus:

> All the nations would say, "Why has the LORD done thus to this land? What means the heat of this great anger?" Then men would say, "It is because they forsook the covenant of the LORD, the God of their fathers, which he made with them when he brought them out of the land of Egypt" (29:24f.).

In that same context we also read that "the LORD has not given you a mind to understand, or eyes to see, or ears to hear" (29:4). Israel was not observant of what God had done for them during the days of the exodus, since on the one hand they were not able to do so because God withheld from them the understanding of mind, yet on the other hand it was because of their forsaking the LORD their God and serving the gods of the neighbors round about them.

257

From this brief survey of Old Testament instances it becomes abundantly clear that the process of the hardening of the heart, whether it be of Pharaoh or of Israel, is a very complex activity in which the LORD and Pharaoh or Israel participate. It is not to be wondered at that devout students have sought to relieve this difficulty, as indeed the first translators of the Hebrew Scriptures did in their rendering of Isaiah 6, in which the prophet is told to bring about the blindness of eyes and deafness of ears and hardness of heart. In the Septuagint this passage reads,

> For this people's heart has grown dull, and their ears are heavy of hearing, and their eyes they have closed, lest they should perceive with their eyes, and hear with their ears, and understand with their heart, and turn for me to heal them (6:10).

This suggests that it is not the prophet who causes the people's unreceptivity, but rather that Israel brings a dull heart and heaviness of hearing and blindness of eyes upon herself.

Since it is quoted in the New Testament, this passage will serve to bring our study into the New Testament. In the Gospel of Matthew Jesus uses the prophet's word to explain his use of parables in which the disciples are permitted to know the secrets of the Kingdom of Heaven, but the people are not so permitted (13:15). To describe this kind of condition which obtained in his own day, Jesus quotes the prophecy of Isaiah. The form of the text is according to the Septuagint, in which the people themselves have brought on their own hardness of heart. In this instance, their hardness

258

of heart prevents them from understanding the secrets of the Kingdom of Heaven. Similarly, the apostle Paul appeals to this same passage to declare that the Holy Spirit was right in describing the unbelieving Jews whom he encountered at Rome (Acts 28:25-27).

The most interesting, if not most difficult, use of the Isaiah passage appears in John's Gospel to explain the Jews' refusal to believe in Jesus (12:37-40). Verses 39 and 40 read, "Therefore they could not believe. For Isaiah again said, 'He has blinded their eyes and hardened their heart, lest they should see with their eyes and perceive with their heart, and turn for me to heal them.' "

The refusal to believe, according to *this* version of the Isaiah text, is brought on by God, who has blinded the eyes and hardened the hearts. One wonders from what source this citation is taken, since it is neither the Massoretic text nor the Septuagint rendering. Perhaps it is a free recall from memory, or more likely an interpretive rendering of the Old Testament passage. Perhaps an undertone from Deuteronomy (referred to above), in which God brings on blindness and deafness, and which has peculiar relevance in the time of Jesus and his appeal to the Jews to accept him, is here attributed to Isaiah.[2]

The problem of the hardening of the heart is most openly taken up by the apostle Paul in Romans 9-11. It is clearly stated in chapter 9:17-18,

> For the scripture says to Pharaoh, "I have raised you up for the very purpose of showing my power in you, so that my name may be proclaimed in all

259

the earth." So then he has mercy upon whomever he wills, and he hardens the heart of whomever he wills.

It seems clear from this that Paul refers to the Old Testament account of the hardening of Pharaoh's heart to establish the obvious conclusion that God and Pharaoh both participated in this matter. Further, Paul wants to make it clear that God exercised mercy toward his people Israel. As in the old dispensation, so also now in the new age, the hardening of heart as manifested by the Jews in rejecting the Gospel comes under the same divine-human activity. Further, Paul appeals to Isaiah 29:10, as we have done in our summary of the Old Testament material, to explain God's part in the hardening phenomenon.

What then? Israel failed to obtain what it sought. The elect obtained it, but the rest were hardened. As it is written,
"God gave them a spirit of stupor,
eyes that should not see and ears that should not hear,
down to this very day" (Rom. 11:7-8).

All this offers the background for a declaration that "a hardening has come upon part of Israel, until the full number of the Gentiles come in" (11:25). These citations are not intended to demonstrate the arbitrariness of God, nor to establish the teaching of predestination, but rather to make clear that God will finally manifest his mercy so that all Israel will be saved. Further, to enlarge the concept of God's mercy Paul adds, "For God has consigned all men to disobedience, that he may have mercy upon all" (11:32). This "all" includes Israel in her hardened heart, as well as Gentiles in their former disobedience.

In summary, our survey of the Old and New Testament data abundantly shows that the process of the hardening of the heart is an activity in which both God and man participate. Further, it is brought to our attention not as some philosophical or theological speculation, but rather in the context of showing mercy to bring about salvation. It should be especially noted that the hardening of the heart takes place in the historical process of God's redemptive purpose to deliver his people from bondage and to establish his covenant with them. As we now go into a survey of interpretation on this matter, it will be evident that many of the church fathers read the Bible not in terms of this historical process of salvation, but rather in terms of establishing a theological or philosophical system.

The History of Interpretation

The Septuagint translation, already mentioned above, is the first to reckon with the problem of the hardening of the heart, for the Hebrew text which makes the prophet the agent of this process of hardening was altered to read that "the people themselves" were responsible for their own hardening. These people, in listening to the prophet, hardened their own hearts, stopped their own ears, and closed their own eyes so that they would not repent and turn to God for healing.

261

Jewish scholars sensed that the passage of Exodus 10:1, which reads, "I have hardened his heart," might lead the heretic to think that he has no responsibility to do penance, since God has hardened the heart. Rabbi Schim'on ben Laqisch replies that the mouth of this heretic can be closed up. In an appeal to Proverbs 3:35, which says that "to the scorner, God is scornful," the comment of this rabbi continues to say that when God warns man once, twice, or three times, and man does not repent, then God closes his heart against future repentance to punish him for whatever sins he has done. The question is asked, what does it mean, "I have hardened the heart"? The answer is seen in a play on the verb which means to harden. This verb also is the word for the noun "liver"; consequently, to harden means to make the heart into a liver, and a liver which, if cooked for the second time, becomes very hard. So it is that Pharaoh's heart became a liver.[3]

Among the early church fathers, we note that Origen maintains that God in his foreknowledge knew that Pharaoh would harden his heart. On the other hand, man has a free will to determine what he will do. It is not, therefore, that God hardens whomever he wills; rather, he hardens whoever refuses to submit in patience to him. So it is that Pharaoh brings on his own stubbornness of heart.

Others like Ambrosius and Pelagius assert that God both grants his mercy and sends his wrath upon the rebellious because of his foreknowledge.

Augustine declares that this interpretation of

foreknowledge is foreign to Paul. According to this Latin father, mankind is a *massa damnata,* a condemned whole. It is an act of mercy, therefore, when God delivers anyone from this damnation, and it is an act of righteousness when he visits his wrath upon those in rebellion and sin. The hardness of heart is Pharaoh's guilt and should not be ascribed to God, who brought it upon him. If one finds this at variance with Paul's teaching, then the church father declares that this is an eternal secret into which man has no right to inquire. God's choice of one or hardening of the other is within his sovereign mystery, before which we are to bow in reverence and thanksgiving.

In conclusion, the early church fathers manifest some uneasiness about the teaching of Paul on the matter of the hardening of the heart. These fathers are especially concerned about maintaining the free will of man, which a declaration of God's hardening the heart seems to negate. Some resort to the foreknowledge of God, which appears to be a mild predestination, to escape the dilemma of a merciful God responsible for man's hardened heart. However, interpreting this matter in terms of the foreknowledge of God is hardly the view of the apostle Paul, who openly declares that God has mercy on the one and hardens the other. We observe that the main concern of many of the fathers is to interpret Paul in theologically or philosophically acceptable categories, whereas the Old Testament, and Paul as well, are concerned with the historical involvement of God in bringing about deliverance of Israel from Egypt on the one hand, or, on the other hand, in bringing the Jews to accept God's final deliverance in Jesus Christ.[4]

Since the scholars of the Reformation follow the classical thought pattern of the early church, the exegesis of passages dealing with our subject becomes especially concerned with the theological and philosophical understanding of God's so-called eternal decrees. In Calvin's thought the *decretum absolutum* allows the sovereign power of God to illumine some to be saved and to harden others to perish. The decrees of God have established whatever the being and doing, the purpose and thinking, of man shall be. Thus, Calvin declares, it is frivolous to ascribe the hardening process to a foreknowledge of God as some early fathers did. The hardening of the heart is ordained by God's sovereign will to be the instrument of his wrath. Calvin, however, manifests uneasiness in affirming that God hardens some for reprobation. This he calls the *decretum horribile*.[5] However, he assures the believer that the divine decrees will result in the great glory of God.

Luther's comments on our subject have been well surveyed in a study by Walther von Loewenich.[6] The main thrust of Luther's thesis is that predestination is the expression of God's will for reconciliation as revealed in Jesus Christ. In choosing his people, God demonstrates his mercy so that we must accept predestination as the occasion for confessing our sin and for acknowledging God's grace. Luther does not choose to discuss the validity of the eternal decree to reprobation and consequently is inclined to bypass the problem of the hardening of the heart by God.

I find myself attracted to Luther's emphasis in making God's mercy and favor primary in the interpretation of the hardening of Pharaoh's heart. In the instance of Pharaoh's hardening of heart Israel was to observe that God acted to bring deliverance. Deliverance did not depend on Israel's will or action, but only on God's mercy.

Some summary statements on the matter will be informative as to how Luther labors with the problem of hardening the heart. (1) He warns against speculation about election and reprobation. (2) When we are troubled about God's hardening Pharaoh's heart, we place God within our rules of right and wrong. God, however, is above law or without law. (3) The matter of hardening must be seen in the historical acts of God and not regarded as God's eternal rejection of the one hardened. (4) Luther rejects Erasmus' teaching that "to harden" is the equivalent of "to give the occasion for hardening," which removes God from the process. Luther stoutly maintains that God is involved. (5) These passages about the hardening of Pharaoh's heart are given for our comfort so that in our temptation we may know that we are in the hands of God. Von Loewenich finds Luther defending the sovereign grace of God which needs no rational explanation as problems of reprobation or hardening of heart arise. Rational process gives way to comforting faith in God's goodness.

Post-reformation scholars, in their comments

on Romans 9:15ff., manifest special concern about the attributes of God, but do not observe that the activity of God in salvation history has high priority both in Romans, and in the Old Testament where the Apostle rightly found it. How does Paul answer the objection in verse 19, "Why does he still find fault? Who can resist his will?" If the answer is in the context of God's eternal decrees, then man has no right to challenge God (ver. 20). If, however, the answer is to be found in the Old Testament potter-clay figure, then Paul points to the historical redemptive activity of God to make clear that God made vessels for beauty and for menial (secondary) use in this activity. Post-reformation scholars are preoccupied with philosophical concepts rather than with the historical process of salvation.[7]

Summary Conclusions

Our survey of the history of interpretation manifests a variety of solutions for the difficulty arising from God's involvement in the hardening of man's heart. We can appreciate the aversion for stating that God in fact hardens the heart. Since the main emphasis of the Scripture is to make God's outgoing love for wayward mankind clear, any idea contrary to this appears to be foreign to the design of Scripture. Yet such foreign designs do appear.

Further, our survey should warn us against finding interpretations that satisfy all the passages under our study, or that will appeal to everyone reading this study. The complexities inherent in the God-man encounter cannot be condensed into simple statements. However, no matter how complex or difficult our task may be, we strive for some understanding of long-standing problems so that we may speak meaningfully in our use of the Scripture, and especially that we may have proper attitudes toward "hardened hearts." Karl L. Schmidt has given a discerning observation:

> The self-hardening of man as his hardening by God, the guilt and responsibility of man as self-judgment and yet also God's judgment, is so complex a matter, affecting the whole man, that there are hardly enough terms to give an adequate spiritual portrayal of the reality of his inner condition. . . . What has the last word is not a theory of predestination but the divine history of salvation in the elect people, a history which just because it is so serious can become a history of judgment and rejection, yet in such a way that finally God in his freedom remains faithful to the rejected and the elect are constantly admonished not to slip back into the way of the rejected. . . . There is always a fear of saying either too much or too little. If we seem to have here a kaleidoscope of harsher and softer colors, the basic color is clearly the beautiful one of the glory of God. Any theory which over-hastily encloses man's sin in the divine action will either run into Gnostic dualism in its attempt to avoid an intolerable monism or commend a quietistic withdrawal in which man finds excuse for his impotence.[8]

Paul in Romans 9-11 neither softened nor explained this prophetic message of hardening. He simply repeated and underlined it. The meaning is, then, not only that this Israel was hardened by

267

God, chapter 11:7-10, but also that on its own responsibility it chose the wrong path, chapter 9:30-10:3. Paul includes a hope for the conversion of hardened Israel, 11:33-36. This conversion is again hoped for both as a human decision (if they do not persist in unbelief, 11:23) and also as a divine act (11:15, life from the dead).[9]

If we seek from Scripture a philosophical statement or propositional truths about God and hope to develop a rational description of God, then we are requesting the Bible to give us help contrary to its basic purpose. However, if we regard the sacred record as the revelation of God's activity of redemption in history, we see the patterns of God's sovereign freedom and of his redemptive grace that illumines the divine-human encounter.

Much of the difficulty that has plagued interpretation has been the inability or unwillingness of Christian exegetes to reckon with the nature of a narrative that cannot be compressed into a well-ordered, rational system. Rather, the biblical narrative deals with the living encounter of God with men and with God's purpose to direct all parts of the God-man involvement into his glorious design of salvation.

Any reflection on the subject of the hardening of the heart or the blinding of the eyes easily becomes enmeshed in the *cause* of this condition of man and the *guilt* developing out of it. The line of thought goes something like this: If indeed God brings about the condition of the hardened heart, then Pharaoh in the account of Exodus, or the

Jews in Paul's discussion in Romans, cannot be held guilty. The problem of cause and consequent guilt, as Paul surmised, would naturally follow from his declaration, "So then he has mercy upon whomever he wills, and he hardens the heart of whomever he wills" (Rom. 9:18). Paul then antici- pates the cause-guilt problem, "You will say to me then, 'Why does he still find fault? For who can resist his will?' " (ver. 19).

Paul's answer to that query is hardly that man has no right to challenge God, but rather that we must properly understand the action of God in the Old Testament history. The accounts of God choosing Jacob rather than Esau, or raising up Pharaoh, which includes the hardening of the heart, or making two kinds of vessels (the one for honor, the other for menial use) are not concerned with the cause-guilt problem, but rather designed to make clear God's sovereign freedom and his re- demptive grace in the course of Israel's history.[10] Paul therefore quiets the raised objection by urg- ing the objector to discern the free flow of God's grace over a lost world.

If we may thus understand the revelation of God in the Old Testament, then our various at- tempts to justify God's involvement in the harden- ing of man's heart are rendered unnecessary. We have noted the attempts of well-intentioned ex- egetes who stated that man hardened his own heart, or that the devil is God's agent for this task,[11] or (to refer to Erasmus) that God gives the occasion for the hardening process. Other attempts could be enumerated. In these noble endeavors to justify God I am reminded of Job's taunt to his friends that they were speaking falsely and deceitfully for God (13:7). I fear that Job would similarly taunt those defending God against Paul's open declaration that "he hardens the heart of whomever he wills." Happily we need not fear Job's taunt if we follow Paul's example not to make the cause-guilt problem our primary concern. J. Moltmann has stated this well:

> The proper understanding of hardening is not in isolating the cause or guilt question but rather in its connection with the eschatological force of divine history. Hardening takes place through God just as reckoning of guilt for hardening is ascribed to man as self-hardening in which separation from God takes place. The historical interweaving of divine activity and human guilt first obtains meaningfulness by understanding the purpose of divine action. The design of the hardening of Israel's enemy or of Israel herself is not the hardening itself but the universal mercy of God. If, however, the Christian is warned against hardening, this warning thus is set in the plane of eschatological hardening since that activity which the Christian opposes is not an internal activity of God but an eschatological unsurpassable activity of God.[12]

The witness of God's redemptive acts in the Old Testament encompasses both the hardening of the heart and, more especially, the opening of the heart;[13] both the blinding of the eyes and the opening of the eyes; both causing Israel to turn from God and bringing Israel back to God. The LORD who is described as hardening the heart is also the one who implants a new heart within Israel (Ezek.

270

36:26), who writes his law upon Israel's heart (Jer. 31:33), who circumcises their hearts that they may love the LORD their God with all their heart and with all their soul that they may live (Deut. 30:6). Let me state the matter carefully: The Old Testament declares that in truth God at times brings on the hardening of heart in Egypt or in Israel; nevertheless, God's persistent concern is to change the hardened heart of people. In the face of Israel's constant rebellion and waywardness, the LORD in his steadfast love reaches out to his people to restore them to their place within the covenant. Through prophet and psalmist, by threats of doom or entreaties of mercy, in times of calamity or prosperity, God pursues his purpose to bring about full redemption for his people. The Old Testament closes with that purpose unrealized. Yet prophets reached into the future with the hope that the God of Israel's redemption would fully establish his design of salvation.

This Old Testament theme of God's unrelenting will and steadfast love inspired Paul in his sorrow and anguish of heart for his fellow Jews. It is true, Paul declares, that a hardening has come upon part of Israel in that they do not confess Jesus as Lord. However, Paul never lets go of the Old Testament future hope that God in his unmerited favor will break the hardened heart after the full number of Gentiles has come in so that all Israel will be saved (Rom. 11:25-26). The Old Testament message of God's undying mercy for Israel furnished Paul with a confident hope for his kinsmen, his own flesh and blood. Thus it is that

Paul is not overcome with the problem of the hardening of the heart because he has learned to trust in the faithfulness of God and in his overflowing favor toward his people.

A chapter on a difficult theme like this can become what the preacher described as "a weariness of the flesh." To relieve that weariness, let me suggest something for our practical pastoral ministry. Let us catch what Paul caught from the Old Testament: a persistent, patient interest in and concern for people, especially for those who appear hardened or turned off. We are instinctively drawn to warmhearted, openminded people and have no difficulty ministering to them, and we understandably bypass the indifferent, the hostile, and the bitter. If we have taken hold of the faithfulness of God, if we have caught the pastoral love of Christ, if we have sensed the inspiring love and devotion of Paul, then we will work untiringly, steadily, and graciously with all, and especially with the hardened heart. If God saw future possibilities in Israel, we ought to see possibilities in our people—even in those who seem to be far removed from us.[14]

I would like to close this study with a quote from Professor Paul Althaus:

> The enigma of the different courses in history of the individual and of the people, of agreement and opposition in being open and being closed to the Word of God, bothers us. We know the design is set in the gracious will of God which is not within our comprehension here on earth. . . . A theology of history which illumines the events and can point out the great design of the divine call and of passing over, that theology is denied us

as long as we ourselves are on the way. We only know in faith that the final disclosing of the will of God moves us like Paul to worship. We lose ourselves in worship since it is of God that the freedom and glory of his love will therein be revealed.[15]

We can well join Paul in his doxology, found in Romans 11:33, 36, "O the depth of the riches and wisdom and knowledge of God! How unsearchable are his judgments and how inscrutable his ways! . . . For from him and through him and to him are all things. To him be the glory forever. Amen."

NOTES

1. Martin Noth has observed that the account in Exodus gives the impression that "from the beginning it was only Yahweh who was really at work"; *Exodus* (London: S.C.M. Press Ltd., 1962), p. 68.

2. See Raymond E. Brown's instructive commentary on this passage, *The Gospel According to John, I-XII*, The Anchor Bible (Garden City, New York: Doubleday and Company, Inc., 1966), pp. 484-86.

3. Strack-Billerbeck, *Kommentar zum Neuen Testament aus Talmud und Midrasch*, vol. 3 (München: C. H. Beck'sche Verlagsbuchhandlung Oskar Beck, 1926), p. 269.

4. Interpretations by early church fathers are well given by Karl H. Schelkle, *Paulus, Lehrer der Väter* (Düsseldorf: Patmos-Verlag, 1956), pp. 341-53. See also Otto Michel, *Der Brief an die Römer* (Göttingen: Vandenhoeck und Ruprecht, 1963), p. 237; W. Sanday and

A. C. Headlam, *The Epistle to the Romans* (New York: Charles Scribner's Sons, 1913), pp. 269-72.

5. John Calvin, *Institutes of the Christian Religion,* III, 23, viii.

6. Walther von Loewenich, "Pharaos Verstockung zu Luthers Lehre von der Prädestination" in *Viva Vox Evangelii, Festschrift für Hans Meiser* (München: Claudius-Verlag, 1951), pp. 196-223.

7. For post-reformation interpretation see F. A. Philippi, *Commentary on the Romans* (Edinburgh: T. and T. Clark, 1879), vol. II, pp. 113-14; also Charles Hodge, *Commentary on the Epistle to the Romans* (New York: A. C. Armstrong and Son, 1896), pp. 459ff.

8. *Theological Dictionary of the New Testament,* vol. V (Grand Rapids: Wm. B. Eerdmans Publishing Co., 1967), p. 1024.

9. *Ibid.,* p. 1027.

10. In Romans 9:20 there is an allusion to Isaiah 45:9 in which the potter-clay figure is used to describe God's relationship to his people. In this context Israel challenges the LORD's use of Cyrus to be his anointed (Messiah!) to deliver Israel from Babylon (45:13). The prophet points out the sovereign freedom of God to bring about salvation in the history of Israel. This idea serves Paul's purpose well to point out God's similar design for Israel of Paul's time, which is that "all Israel will be saved" (Rom. 11:26).

11. An appeal can be made to II Corinthians 4:4, "In their case the god of this world has blinded the minds of the unbelievers, to keep them from seeing the light of the gospel of the glory of Christ."

12. J. Moltmann, *Die Religion in Geschichte und Gegenwart,*[3] VI (Tübingen: J. C. Mohr [Paul Siebeck], 1962), col. 1385.

13. I owe much to G. von Rad's careful treatment of the problem of the hardened heart in his comments on

274

Isaiah (6:9-10; 8:17; 29:9-14). He turns away from the common practice of importing exegesis into the text and insists that the troublesome passage be explored in the full context of the prophet. The hardening of the heart is not the final word, for the creative powerful Word of the LORD will indeed create a new and responsive heart. Thus, it is not necessary to labor the problem of the cause of the hardened heart, for the creative Word, which directs redemptive history, also works within mankind. *Old Testament Theology,* vol. II (New York: Harper and Row, 1965), pp. 151-55.

14. Formal treatment of our subject is found in: Karl L. Schmidt in "Die Verstockung des Menschen durch Gott: Eine lexikologische und biblische-theologische Studie," *Theologische Zeitschrift* (1945), pp. 1-17; Franz Hesse in "Das Verstockungsproblem im Alten Testament," Beihefte ZAW, 74 (1955).

15. Paul Althaus, *Die Christliche Wahrheit* (Gütersloh: Carl Bertelsmann Verlag, 1962), pp. 629-30.

SUMMARY COMMENT

THIS STUDY OF THE RELATIONSHIP BETWEEN THE
Old and New Testaments was undertaken with
the hope of finding a method which would help
Christians make a proper and effective use of the
Old Testament. Any study that takes into account
all the material of the Old Testament will encounter some problem in determining how to devise a
method that can be used to make the ancient
Scripture a living word for our present age. From
the first the author has been aware of the problem
inherent in the Old Testament itself, a problem already recognized by the writers of the New Testament. Consequently he has been under no illusions
of finding a solution or solutions that would put
all questions at rest. However, rather than curse
the darkness of the problem, to borrow a Chinese
proverb, it has seemed more sensible to light a
candle which may shed a little light for our understanding and use of the Old Testament.

The reader will note that this book does not
take up the difficulties mentioned in Chapter II
concerning the Old Testament which have caused
some scholars to give those ancient writings a non-

canonical or a secondary rating. These difficulties become especially annoying for those who attempt to devise statements on the inspiration of the Bible which will do justice to all the data of the Bible. The author's design, which may either reflect a lack of courage or a sagacity unwitting and unlooked for, was not to discuss the problem of inspiration. The purpose was rather more practical: to make the Old Testament more usable. Or—to call attention to the title, *The Scripture Unbroken* as discussed in the Foreword—to attempt to answer the question in what way and to what degree does the Old Testament have validity today?

The principle of selectivity played an important role in the writing of this book; and moreover this principle takes on significant importance regarding our search for a method for using the Old Testament. We need not apologize for this since the writers of the New Testament were selective in their use of the Scripture as was pointed out in Chapter I. They concentrated their attention on certain sections, and within these parts they made special choice of what they considered to be fulfilled and to be valid and authoritative for the church, the community of the new covenant. Furthermore, throughout the history of the church, whether in choosing some rule of interpretation, or in accepting some parts as valid and authoritative and in rejecting others, or in finding passages to support an a priori system of doctrine, selectivity in one form or another was very prominent, as Chapter II intimates. An admission that selectivity has been a part of our method would indicate that we have learned from the past, and that we speak with integrity about our use of the Scriptures.

The selection of subjects discussed in the foregoing chapters was in part dictated by the practical consideration of keeping the book within convenient length. It is hoped, however, that these chapters deal with the essentials which comprise God's redemptive purpose in the Old Testament. Further, it is hoped that the message of the Old Testament may be seen in its New Testament fulfillment so that thereby we may honor the "unbrokenness" of the Scripture.

Subjects not discussed in this book await the earnest probing of such readers who may be inspired to do this. They will discover that the law and the prophets related to and modified by the epistles and gospels contain much that can be represented in messages important for our times. Jesus' counsel to "search the scriptures" (Jn. 5:39) should urge us to do careful research in various parts of the Old Testament. As this research comes to involve our personal commitment to arrive at a proper understanding of what the Old Testament presents, we shall encounter a living word which takes on more life as it finds completion in the New Testament. The light of the Old Testament reaches its intended beauty and brilliance when seen in the face of Jesus Christ (II Cor. 4:6).

INDEX OF BIBLICAL
REFERENCES

282